D1640061

REGARDS
ANSICHTEN
REFLECTIONS

Himalaya

Erhard Loretan

**REGARDS
ANSICHTEN
REFLECTIONS**

Erhard Loretan — Himalaya

ÉDITIONS LA SARINE
PAULUSVERLAG

Autre titre:

Erhard Loretan. Les 8000 rugissants
Erhard Loretan et Jean Ammann

Editions La Sarine, 1996
ISBN 2-88355-029-8

Früher erschienen:

Erhard Loretan. Den Bergen verfallen
Erhard Loretan und Jean Ammann
Übersetzung: Christine Kopp
Paulusverlag, 1996
ISBN 3-7228-0396-9

**Aus dem Französischen übersetzt
von Christine Kopp**

© 1998, Editions La Sarine, Fribourg

Concept, réalisation et impression:
Imprimerie Saint-Paul, Fribourg, Suisse

Brochage: Schumacher SA, Schmitten

ISBN 2-88355-038-7 (La Sarine)

© 1998, Paulusverlag, Freiburg

Gestaltung, Satz und Druck:
Paulusdruckerei, Freiburg, Schweiz

Einband: Schumacher AG, Schmitten

ISBN 3-7228-0442-6 (Paulusverlag)

Translated from the French by Trevor Braham

A mon cher ami Ruedi
et à tous ceux qui m'ont permis
de réaliser mes rêves

Meinem lieben Freund Ruedi
und allen, die es mir ermöglicht haben,
meine Träume zu verwirklichen

To my friend Ruedi
and to all those who have enabled me
to fulfil my dreams

Introduction

Qu'y a-t-il de plus enthousiasmant pour un jeune que de découvrir une passion qui le comblera durant toute son existence? Etre alpiniste, n'est-ce pas le meilleur moyen de se rapprocher du ciel tant physiquement que spirituellement?

Cette expérience de la passion, j'ai eu la chance de la vivre. La montagne m'a complètement envoûté alors que j'étais très jeune, si bien que rapidement je n'ai eu plus que des images d'altitude en tête. Et chaque instant de liberté, je l'ai consacré à ma passion. Les programmes scolaires ne me motivaient guère. La raison en était simple: j'étais convaincu que je deviendrais guide professionnel. J'estimais alors que la vie m'apprendrait par elle-même ce qui allait m'être utile. J'étais néanmoins tout à fait conscient que ce métier n'était pas sans risques et qu'il pouvait être subitement interrompu. Rien n'était moins sûr que de pouvoir vivre de cette passion. Raison pour laquelle je m'appliquai à apprendre un premier métier, celui d'ébéniste.

Einführung

Gibt es für einen jungen Menschen etwas Begeisternderes, als eine Leidenschaft zu entdecken, die ihn sein ganzes Leben lang erfüllen wird? Wie könnte man dem Himmel – körperlich und geistig – besser nahekommen denn als Alpinist?

Ich hatte das Glück, in meinem Leben eine solche Leidenschaft kennenzulernen: Ich war noch sehr jung, als mich die Berge vollständig in ihren Bann zogen – so sehr, dass ich bald nur noch Bilder aus höheren Gegenden im Kopf hatte und jeden freien Augenblick meiner Leidenschaft widmete. Die Schule interessierte mich aus einem einfachen Grund herzlich wenig: Ich wollte Bergführer werden und dachte, das Leben werde mir von selbst beibringen, was ich brauchte. Ich war mir aber auch völlig bewusst, dass die Ausübung dieses Berufs mit Risiken verbunden ist und unversehens unterbrochen werden kann. Ich hätte nichts Unsichereres wählen können, als meine Leidenschaft zu leben.

Introduction

What could give keener joy to a young person than to discover a fulfilling and lifelong passion? Is there not no better way to reach the skies – physically and spiritually – than as a mountaineer?

It has been my good fortune to experience a passion for the mountains, which has shaped my life. Ever since I was very young the mountains cast a magical spell over me, so much so that soon visions of high peaks began to push all other thoughts out of my mind. Every free moment that I could find was devoted to my passion. Lessons taught in the schoolroom failed to motivate me. The reason was quite clear. I had made up my mind to become a professional guide, and I felt that my future life would teach me everything that I needed to know. I was fully aware of the risks involved in my chosen profession. Nothing seemed to be less secure than my chosen way of life. It did not seem to offer a secure livelihood.

Je dois avouer avoir vécu alors une période difficile. Tous les matins, je me levais la boule à l'estomac, non pas que le métier ne me convenait pas, au contraire, mais les conditions d'apprentissage étaient telles qu'à la simple idée de devoir retourner quotidiennement sur ma place de travail, j'en devenais malade. Au milieu des années septante, on vivait des temps économiquement difficiles. Si bien qu'il était impensable de changer de profession. Et pourtant, un jour j'ai pris mon courage à deux mains et j'ai posé mon bleu de travail, au risque de ne pas achever mon apprentissage. Dès l'instant où j'ai quitté l'atelier, ma vie a changé; j'étais soudainement heureux. Heureusement tout de même, j'ai eu la chance de trouver un nouvel employeur, avec qui je me suis bien entendu et qui m'a permis de terminer ma formation.

Mon pénible service obligatoire à la patrie terminé, je décidai de changer ma vie. Je n'avais plus qu'une envie: découvrir les montagnes du monde. Quelle chance de pouvoir vivre en ne sachant pas de quoi le lendemain serait fait! La vie deviendrait alors tellement plus excitante.

Tenter l'ascension d'un 8000 m était un rêve qui m'avait effleuré l'esprit dès l'âge de quinze ans. Deux ans plus tard, avec des amis, j'entrepris des démarches officielles afin d'organiser une expédition au Nanga Parbat (8125 m). Le livre de Hermann Buhl nous avait mis l'eau à la bouche. Mais il fallut encore patienter, plusieurs chicanes nous empêchant de réaliser notre rêve. Et c'est en 1982 que ce rêve un peu fou se réalisa enfin. L'ascension du Nanga Parbat se fit selon une méthode conventionnelle. Nous avions équipé la montagne en y plaçant quelques cordes et quatre camps fixes. Il s'agissait de se tester,

Deshalb bemühte ich mich, einen ersten Beruf – jenen des Möbelschreiners – zu erlernen.

Zugegeben, ich habe dann eine schwierige Zeit erlebt: Der Beruf sagte mir zwar zu, doch wenn ich nur schon daran dachte, täglich zur Arbeit zu gehen, wurde ich krank und bekam Magenschmerzen – schuld daran waren die Verhältnisse während meiner Lehre. Mitte der siebziger Jahre herrschten wirtschaftlich schwierige Zeiten, und es wäre undenkbar gewesen, den Beruf zu wechseln. Und doch nahm ich eines Tages all meinen Mut zusammen und gab meine Arbeitskleider ab – auf die Gefahr hin, meine Lehre nicht beenden zu können. Von dem Moment an, wo ich die Werkstatt verliess, veränderte sich mein Leben: Ich war auf einmal glücklich. Zugleich hatte ich das Glück, einen neuen Arbeitgeber zu finden, mit dem ich mich gut verstand und bei dem ich meine Lehre beenden konnte.

Nachdem ich die Rekrutenschule – meinen mühsamen Dienst am Vaterland – hinter mich gebracht hatte, beschloss ich, mein Leben zu ändern. Ich hatte nur auf eines Lust: die Berge der Welt zu entdecken. Welch ein Glück, leben zu können, ohne zu wissen, was der nächste Tag bringt! Das Leben ist damit so viel spannender …

Seit meinem fünfzehnten Lebensjahr träumte ich davon, einmal einen Achttausender zu besteigen. Zwei Jahre später unternahm ich zusammen mit Freunden erste Schritte, um eine Expedition an den Nanga Parbat (8125 m) zu organisieren. Hermann Buhls Buch machte uns den Mund wässerig. Doch wir mussten uns gedulden – erst 1982 gelang es uns, unseren

So I set myself to take up a trade, and to learn the craft of a carpenter.

This period, I have to admit was a very difficult one for me. I used to wake each morning with a feeling of dread. The thought of having to return daily to my work-place sickened me. During the economically difficult years of the mid-1970s it seemed unthinkable to attempt to change one's profession. Nevertheless, taking my courage in both hands I decided one day to abandon my daily work-clothes, placing at risk the opportunity to complete my apprenticeship. From the moment that I left the workshop, my life changed, and I began to sense a feeling of contentment. I was fortunately able to find a new employer with whom I was able to complete my training.

After finishing my tiresome spell of compulsory Army Service, I decided to change the course of my life. I had just one wish: to get to know the world's mountains. A marvellous opportunity to be able to live without a thought for what tomorrow might bring! Life suddenly had become much more exciting.

From the age of 15 the dream of climbing an 8000 m mountain had hovered over my mind. Two years later together with a few friends, we took the first steps to organise an expedition to Nanga Parbat (8125 m). For us Hermann Buhl's book acted as a mouth-watering temptation. But it was necessary to be patient. There were a number of tricks we still had to learn before we could live out our wild dream and it was not until 1982 that we were able to do so. We climbed Nanga Parbat following the conventional Himalayan style, by placing 4 fixed camps, each connected

de savoir si notre corps était vraiment apte à parer au manque d'oxygène. Déjà partisans d'une certaine éthique, nous avions décidé de ne pas engager de porteurs d'altitude et de ne pas recourir à l'oxygène artificiel. Tout se passa très bien pour moi puisque j'atteignis le sommet avec Norbert Joos dans des conditions difficiles, sans que mon organisme n'ait trop souffert.

Ce fut le déclic. Je n'avais plus de raison de m'arrêter en si bon chemin. Je venais d'acquérir la preuve que j'avais «le physique de l'emploi» et que la très haute altitude allait devenir mon domaine privilégié pour tenter de repousser au maximum les limites des possibilités humaines. Les expéditions – au nombre d'une trentaine à ce jour – s'enchaînèrent à un rythme régulier.

Aujourd'hui, si je fais un premier bilan, je peux sans aucun doute affirmer que je suis un homme comblé. La montagne m'a tout donné. S'il s'agissait de tout reprendre à zéro, je n'y changerais rien. J'ai tout simplement l'immense avantage de pouvoir vivre mes rêves.

J'ai conscience que c'est un privilège formidable que de pouvoir vivre des aventures aussi extraordinaires, de voyager à travers le monde à la découverte d'autres cultures, d'autres gens, d'autres façons de vivre et de penser.

En parcourant le monde et en vivant des situations extrêmes, on perçoit avec un certain recul les problèmes qui caractérisent notre société dite civilisée, qui bute trop souvent sur des futilités et qui fait preuve parfois d'étroitesse d'esprit.

Je me suis rendu compte que la richesse ou la pauvreté n'est qu'un état, qui ne se mesure pas

etwas verrückten Traum zu verwirklichen und den Nanga Parbat im damals üblichen Stil zu besteigen: Wir brachten am Berg ein paar Fixseile an und richteten vier feste Lager ein. Die Besteigung sollte uns zeigen, ob unser Körper die sauerstoffarme Luft wirklich vertrug. Wir wendeten bei unseren Unternehmungen bereits eine gewisse Ethik an und verzichteten deshalb auf die Anstellung von Hochträgern und den Einsatz von Sauerstoffflaschen. Bei mir passte alles zusammen: Ohne dass mein Organismus allzu sehr litt, erreichte ich, bei schwierigen Verhältnissen, den Gipfel zusammen mit Norbert Joos.

Das war der eigentliche Auslöser: Nun, da ich einmal in Schwung geraten war, gab es keinen Grund, anzuhalten. Eben hatte ich den Beweis erlangt, dass ich mich für das «Metier» eignete und die extreme Höhe zu meinem bevorzugten Gelände werden würde, in dem ich die Grenzen der menschlichen Möglichkeiten so weit wie möglich hinauszuschieben versuchte. Die Expeditionen – bis heute sind es ungefähr dreissig – folgten sich von nun an in regelmässigem Rhythmus.

Ziehe ich heute ein erstes Mal Bilanz, so kann ich sagen: Ich bin ein erfüllter Mensch. Die Berge haben mir alles gegeben. Könnte ich noch einmal von vorne anfangen, so würde ich nichts ändern. Ich habe einfach die grosse Gunst, meine Träume leben zu können.

Ich bin mir bewusst, dass es ein wunderbares Privileg ist, solch aussergewöhnliche Abenteuer zu erleben und auf der Entdeckung von anderen Kulturen, anderen Menschen, anderen Lebens- und Denkarten durch die Welt zu reisen.

to the other by a route secured with fixed ropes. It was important to find out how our bodies would react to an atmosphere deficient in oxygen. We had made up our minds to adopt certain ethical principles, rejecting the use of artificial oxygen and high altitude porters. It was a wonderful experience for me, because N. Joos and I reached the summit under fairly difficult conditions, which left me physically unaffected.

That was what really set me going. Having tread on this wholly delightful path, there seemed to be no further reason for me to hesitate. It had been proved to me that my physique had just what it takes, and that I was free to enter the privileged world of extreme altitudes and push myself to the limits of human capacity. My subsequent expeditions – 30 in all so far – began to follow a regular pattern.

Today, if I were to weigh up my experiences, I would say without the slightest doubt that I am a deeply fulfilled person. The mountains have given me all that I ever wanted. If I were to start again from the beginning, I would wish to change nothing. Quite simply, I have been immensely fortunate to have been able to live my dreams.

I feel that I am tremendously privileged to have experienced a number of extraordinary adventures, to have travelled across the world, coming into contact with a variety of people of other cultures and with different ways of life and thought.

Travelling through various countries of the world and being involved in extreme situations enables one to react in a different way to some

en argent mais en bonheur intérieur. Je me suis aperçu que les choses faciles n'ont aucune saveur. Ce sont les moments les plus difficiles qui vous remplissent le cœur et l'esprit. Ils se transforment en vos plus beaux souvenirs. J'ai l'impression que je vis en quelques jours «là-haut» ce que j'aurais de la peine à vivre en plusieurs années «en bas».

Au gré de mes expériences, je suis devenu très fataliste. J'ai pris le parti de vivre intensément, en côtoyant le risque. Je préfère une existence courte et dynamique à une vie longue mais terne. On me demande constamment pourquoi je grimpe, la réponse se trouve dans les images composant ce livre… Après trente ans d'extraordinaires aventures, il était temps de faire partager quelques images à ceux qui n'ont pas la chance de les vivre. Même si elles ne représentent qu'un pâle reflet du vécu, elles ouvrent des fenêtres sur… mon vécu.

Auf Reisen und in Extremsituationen hat man einen gewissen Abstand zu den Problemen unserer sogenannt zivilisierten Gesellschaft, die zu oft über Belanglosigkeiten stolpert – was manchmal das Zeichen einer gewissen Kleinkariertheit ist.

Ich habe erkannt, dass Reichtum und Armut lediglich Zustände sind, die sich nicht in Geld, sondern in innerem Glück messen lassen. Alles, was zu leicht gelingt, ist – wie meine Erfahrung mir gezeigt hat – völlig ohne Reiz; vielmehr sind es die schwierigsten Momente, die Herz und Geist erfüllen: Sie verwandeln sich in die schönsten Erinnerungen. Was ich «dort oben» in ein paar Tagen erlebe, sammle ich «hier unten» in mehreren Jahren nur mit Mühe an.

Durch meine Erfahrungen bin ich sehr fatalistisch geworden. Ich habe mich für ein intensives Leben nahe an der Gefahr entschieden. Ich ziehe ein kurzes, dynamisches Leben einem langen, aber dumpfen und eintönigen Dasein vor.

Ich werde immer wieder gefragt, weshalb ich in die Berge gehe – die Antwort steht in den Bildern dieses Buchs… Es ist Zeit, einige dieser Bilder mit jenen Menschen zu teilen, die das Glück nicht haben, ebenso aussergewöhnliche Abenteuer zu erleben, wie ich es in den letzten dreissig Jahren tun konnte. Auch wenn die Aufnahmen nur der blasse Abglanz des Erlebten sind, öffnen sie Fenster… auf mein Leben!

of the problems common to our so-called civilised society, which often occupies itself in futile activities and too often displays a narrowness of spirit.

It has often occured to me that wealth and poverty are not more than a state of mind, not measurable in terms of money, but present in one's inner being. I have learnt that the easy way does not provide any real satisfaction. It is the hardest moments which are the most fulfilling to the spirit, and which are retained by the mind as the most memorable. The impressions which I have gained in a few days spent high on the peaks could never have been achieved in several more years living below.

My experiences have turned me into something of a fatalist. Living intensely, hand in hand with risk, is my chosen life-style. I prefer a life that may be brief, but powered by vigorous activity, to one that is spiritless and long-lived.

I have often been asked why I climb. My answer is given in the pictures which can be found in this book. Having experienced 30 years of wonderful adventures, it seems to me time to share with others who have been less fortunate some of the glories of the mountain scene. Though they are no more than a pale reflection of the reality – they throw open a window to… my life.

Le village népalais de Ghandrung au pied de l'Annapurna Sud (7219 m) et du Hiunchuli (6441 m).

Das nepalesische Dorf Ghandrung am Fuss der Annapurna Süd (7219 m) und des Hiunchuli (6441 m).

The Nepalese village of Ghandrung at the foot of Annapurna South (7219 m), and Hiunchuli (6441 m).

Une ambiance féerique...
    Märchenhafte Stimmung...
  A magical atmosphere...

Que ce soit à 2000 m ou à 8000 m, l'effet magique des cimes ne s'estompe jamais!
Ob auf 2000 oder auf 8000 Meter: die zauberhafte Wirkung der Gipfel verblasst nie!
Whether at 2000 m or 8000 m the magical effect of the summits never fades.

Les Gastlosen

Les «Gastlosen» – les «inhospitalières» en français – constituent une chaîne de montagnes calcaires. Elles représentent mon terrain de prédilection. C'est là que j'ai passé les plus belles heures de mon temps libre. J'y ai laissé sang et eau. L'exaltation et l'angoisse y ont fait bon ménage. Elles m'ont tant donné que, toujours, je leur resterai fidèle.

Je leur rends visite aussi souvent que possible. De ma terrasse, j'ai la chance de les observer en permanence. A chaque instant, elles offrent des éclats renouvelés. S'il m'arrive de ne plus pouvoir les observer pendant un certain temps, alors elles me manquent.

Je les trahis quelque peu lorsque je pars en expédition, mais elles comprennent que j'ai choisi une voie qui me rend heureux. Les distances n'empêchent pas nos relations de proximité. A chacun de mes retours, notre complicité se consolide.

Die Gastlosen

Die Gastlosen, ein kleines Massiv von Kalkgipfeln, sind mein liebstes Gelände. Hier habe ich meine schönsten freien Stunden verbracht, hier habe ich Blut und Wasser geschwitzt, Begeisterung und Furcht erlebt. Diese Berge haben mir so viel gegeben, dass ich ihnen immer treu bleiben werde.

So oft wie möglich suche ich sie auf. Von meinem Balkon aus sehe ich sie immer – ihr Aussehen wechselt ständig. Wenn ich sie eine Zeitlang nicht mehr betrachten kann, fehlen sie mir.

Ich werde ihnen etwas untreu, wenn ich zu einer Expedition aufbreche – doch sie verstehen, dass ich einen Weg gewählt habe, der mich glücklich macht.

Die Distanz verändert nichts an unserer engen Beziehung. Jedesmal, wenn ich zurückkehre, festigt sich unser geheimes Einverständnis.

The Gastlosen

Gastlosen, a German word meaning inhospitable or forbidding, is the name of a range of limestone mountains situated near my home for which I have a special fondness. It is there that I have spent some of the happiest hours of my life. Amongst its rocks I have shed my blood and sweat and it has been for me an arena both of anguish and of glory. Those mountains have given me so much that I shall always remain devoted to them.

I still visit them as often as I can. From my chalet I have them permanently in view. From one moment to the next, they always seem to provide a different lustre. If, for an interval, I have not been able to see them, I long to see them again.

I feel like a traitor when I leave them to set off on an expedition; but I feel that they understand that I have chosen a course that would give me pleasure. Distance does not interfere with the closeness of our feelings, and each time I return our special connection is strengthened.

Les Gastlosen, de toutes, restent mes préférées.
Die Gastlosen – nach wie vor meine liebsten Berge!
The Gastlosen, which still remain, of all mountains, my favourite.

Avec Jean Troillet, nous venons de renoncer au pilier ouest du Makalu (8463 m). Celui-ci pourtant nous adresse un dernier clin d'œil.
Eben haben Jean Troillet und ich einen Versuch am Westpfeiler des Makalu (8463 m) abgebrochen; doch der Berg lockt uns immer noch…
Makalu 8463 m gives us a last glance as Troillet and I decide to abandon our West Face attempt.

Lorsque la lune côtoie les sommets, la nature dévoile d'autres dimensions. Shisha Pangma (8046 m), Tibet.
Wenn der Mond die Gipfel berührt, enthüllt die Natur andere Dimensionen. Shisha Pangma (8046 m), Tibet.
When the moon approaches the summits nature reveals a different dimension. Shisha Pangma (8046 m), Tibet.

Les règles du jeu

Depuis la première ascension de l'Everest en 1953 par Tenzing et Hillary, l'himalayisme a considérablement évolué. Depuis 1978, date de la première ascension sans oxygène par Messner et Habeler, les alpinistes savent que l'on peut atteindre le «troisième pôle» sans oxygène. Pourtant, rares sont encore ceux qui jouent le jeu.

Je ne suis pas favorable à une interdiction totale de l'utilisation de l'oxygène. Je ne critique pas non plus les expéditions commerciales. Le guide doit bien vivre. En revanche, ce qui me heurte, c'est le manque d'éthique qui caractérise la majorité de ces expéditions.

Il est médicalement établi que le fait de recourir à une bouteille d'oxygène à 8000 m équivaut en fait à vous ramener à une altitude de 6000 m. Il faut donc relativiser les performances de ceux qui recourent à de tels substituts.

Die Spielregeln

Seit der Erstbesteigung des Everest durch Tenzing und Hillary im Jahr 1953 hat das Himalaya-Bergsteigen eine grosse Entwicklung erfahren. Seit 1978, als Messner und Habeler den höchsten Gipfel der Welt – den sogenannten «Dritten Pol» – erstmals ohne künstlichen Sauerstoff bestiegen, weiss man, dass dies überhaupt möglich ist. Allerdings sind jene, die es tun, immer noch die Ausnahme.

Ich bin nicht für ein totales Verbot von Sauerstoffflaschen. Ich kritiere auch die kommerziellen Expeditionen nicht. Der Bergführer soll gut leben können. Was mich aber stört, ist der Mangel an Ethik, der die meisten Expeditionen kennzeichnet.

Wer auf 8000 m künstlichen Sauerstoff verwendet, versetzt sich damit auf eine Höhe von 6000 m – dies ist medizinisch erwiesen; man muss deshalb die Leistungen jener, die auf solche Hilfsmittel zurückgreifen, relativieren.

The rules of the game

After Everest was first climbed in 1953 by Hillary and Tenzing there have been considerable developments in Himalayan climbing. Ever since Messner and Habeler climbed the mountain without using supplementary oxygen in 1978, it has been clear to mountaineers that it is perfectly possible to reach the «Third Pole» without carrying oxygen cylinders; yet even today there are few who do so.

I am not arguing in favour of abandoning the use of oxygen altogether. Nor do I wish to criticize commercial expeditions; mountain guides must live. What strikes me as most objectionable is the lack of ethical behaviour shown by the majority of those expeditions.

According to medical opinion, the use of supplementary oxygen at 8000 m reduces the climbers level to 6000 m in practical terms. Those, therefore, who use this supplementary aid should rate the quality of their performance accordingly.

Urdukas, dernière oasis confortable pour ces porteurs baltis. Une étape lors de la marche d'approche du K2.

Urdukas, letzte bequeme Oase für diese Balti-Träger und Etappenhalt auf dem Anmarsch zum K2.

Urdukas, the last comfortable campsite for Balti porters on the approach march to K2.

La longue route des porteurs
Der lange Weg der Träger
The porters' long journey

Durant deux à trois semaines, ces porteurs deviennent nos compagnons d'aventure.
Ils transportent de lourdes charges dans des conditions souvent extrêmes.

Diese Träger teilen während zwei bis drei Wochen unser Abenteuer;
sie tragen schwere Lasten unter oft extremen Bedingungen.

For a period of two or three weeks these porters share our adventures,
carrying heavy loads under conditions that are often very hard.

Le métier d'alpiniste

Aujourd'hui, la montagne me permet de vivre. Passion et activité professionnelle se mêlent. J'exerce un métier très varié, qui me conduit dans les quatre coins du monde. Je présente mes aventures dans des salles de conférences, je fais de la randonnée avec des néophytes, j'accompagne des alpinistes chevronnés dans de grandes parois, j'effectue des travaux acrobatiques sur des chantiers délicats et je continue à exercer mon premier métier, l'ébénisterie.

J'éprouve toujours un très grand plaisir à raconter mes aventures. A la sortie de mes conférences, j'aime observer mon public, je décèle dans le regard des spectateurs des signes de bonheur. L'espace de deux heures, il se sont évadés au fond de leurs rêves. Pour moi, ce sont des moments très gratifiants.

Lorsque je guide, je retrouve des sensations de grande aventure. Des gens de tout niveau me confient leur vie; cette responsabilité me place face à des situations psychologiques comparables à celles que je côtoie lors de grandes expéditions.

Un jour, je me trouvais avec un Japonais sur la voie normale du Cervin. Il ne parlait pas l'anglais, et moi, le japonais… Mon client n'avait pas beaucoup d'expérience, mais je sentais que cette ascension était très importante pour lui. Je décidai de tout entreprendre pour l'emmener au sommet. Je ne m'étais pas trompé: ce jour fut sans doute le plus beau de sa vie. Il se mit à pleurer comme une «madeleine». Je ne pus m'empêcher de verser une larme, tellement j'étais heureux pour lui.

Der Beruf des Bergsteigers

Heute kann ich von den Bergen leben: Leidenschaft und Beruf ergänzen sich. Ich übe einen sehr vielfältigen Beruf aus, der mich in alle Ecken der Welt führt. Ich halte Vorträge über meine Abenteuer, ich unternehme Wanderungen mit Anfängern, ich begleite erfahrene Alpinisten durch grosse Wände, ich führe Arbeiten auf gefährlichen Baustellen aus und übe daneben weiterhin meinen ersten Beruf, den des Möbelschreiners, aus.

Es ist für mich immer ein grosses Vergnügen, über meine Abenteuer zu erzählen. Am Ende eines Vortrags beobachte ich gerne mein Publikum – und entdecke dabei in den Augen der Zuschauer manchmal Anzeichen von Glück: Während zwei Stunden ziehen sie sich in die Tiefe ihrer Träume zurück… Für mich sind dies sehr erfüllende Augenblicke.

Bei der Arbeit als Bergführer verspüre ich die gleichen Empfindungen wie bei grossen Abenteuern. Menschen von ganz unterschiedlichem Niveau vertrauen mir ihr Leben an; durch diese Verantwortung bin ich mit ähnlichen psychologischen Situationen konfrontiert wie auf grossen Expeditionen.

Einmal führte ich einen Japaner über die Normalroute auf das Matterhorn. Er sprach kein Englisch, und was mein Japanisch angeht – na ja…! Mein Gast hatte keine grosse Erfahrung, aber ich spürte, dass diese Tour für ihn sehr wichtig war. Ich entschloss mich, alles zu unternehmen, um ihn auf den Gipfel zu führen. Und ich täuschte mich nicht: Jener Tag war sicherlich der schönste seines Lebens. Er begann zu weinen wie ein Schlosshund… Und ich war so glücklich für ihn, dass ich selbst eine Träne vergoss!

A mountainer's vocation

Today I have been able to combine my passion with my profession, and the mountains provide me with a living. My activities are as varied as possible, taking me to every corner of the world. My mountain adventures provide me with material for lectures, I lead trekking groups comprising parties of beginners, I accompany experienced mountaineers on classic climbs, I carry out delicate work on exposed building sites, and in addition I continue to practise my profession as a carpenter.

It gives me immense pleasure to present an account of my adventures, and I find it gratifying to observe among the audience evidence of their genuine joy at being able to escape for a couple of hours into a dream-world.

When I am guiding a client, of whatever level of competence who has entrusted me with his life, the responsibility that I feel is the same as that on a major expedition when situations arise of my own choosing, involving similar degrees of psychological intensity.

Once I found myself guiding a Japanese client up the Hörnli ridge (the normal route) of the Matterhorn. He was not an experienced climber, and it was obvious to me that he was desperately keen to make the ascent. I could speak no Japanese, and he hardly any English. I decided to do everything I could to help him to reach the top. We were not outdone. On the summit he shed copious tears of pure joy; it was obviously the happiest day of his life. I was so happy for him that I found my own eyes turning moist.

Arête est de l'Annapurna (8091 m), la plus grande traversée réalisée en haute altitude. Norbert Joss–Erhard Loretan, octobre 1984.
Die bisher längste Überschreitung in extremer Höhe gelang Norbert Joss und Erhard Loretan 1984 am Ostgrat der Annapurna (8091 m).
The East ridge of Annapurna (8091 m) the longest high altitude traverse ever achieved. Norbert Joss, Erhard Loretan October 1984.

Conflit de générations ?

Ces dernières années, l'escalade sportive a pris le pas sur l'alpinisme traditionnel. Il s'agit là de deux disciplines bien différentes, que je tente de concilier. Les itinéraires à la mode sont de plus en plus équipés depuis le haut en redescendant les parois en rappel, ce que je conçois dans le cadre d'écoles d'escalade. En revanche, j'ai plus de peine à l'admettre pour les grandes falaises.

Lorsque j'ai débuté, avec mes amis, nous avons ouvert de nouveaux itinéraires en utilisant le moins d'équipement possible, car telle était l'éthique de l'époque. A l'heure actuelle, je n'ai pas modifié mes méthodes. Les grandes falaises sont équipées depuis le bas, mais les spits ont remplacé les cordelettes et les pitons.

Mes itinéraires ont la réputation d'être peu sûrs et aventureux. Qu'ils soient considérés comme aventureux me rend assez fier. L'escalade sportive n'offre plus l'occasion d'utiliser un piton ou un coinceur dans les écoles. Je ne suis cependant pas opposé à ce que quelques voies, dans un secteur déterminé où évoluent des débutants, soient très bien équipées. Mais il ne faut pas exagérer et respecter tout le monde.

Il est nécessaire de conserver quelques voies à risques à l'intention des alpinistes qui se hasardent encore dans de grandes courses dans les Alpes, en terrain mixte, qui est souvent très exposé et où la chute n'est pas permise.

Je trouve évidemment normal le remplacement de vieux ancrages dans d'anciennes voies. Par contre, je trouve tout à fait déplacé lorsqu'en lieu et place on y installe une forêt de points d'assurage. J'y vois une forme d'incompétence et surtout un manque de respect vis-à-vis des vaillants premiers ascensionnistes.

Generationenkonflikt ?

In den letzten Jahren hat das Sportklettern den traditionellen Alpinismus hinter sich gelassen. Es handelt sich dabei um zwei sehr verschiedene Disziplinen, die ich in Einklang zu bringen versuche. Immer häufiger werden Kletterrouten beim Abseilen eingerichtet – dieses Vorgehen akzeptiere ich beim Einrichten von Klettergärten, aber bei grossen Wänden habe ich damit Mühe.

Als ich mit meinen Freunden zu klettern begann, eröffneten wir – entsprechend der Ethik jener Zeit – Neutouren mit möglichst wenig Material. Bis heute habe ich meine Methoden nicht geändert. Grosse Wände werden von unten eingerichtet, aber statt Bohrhaken verwende ich Reepschnüre und Haken.

Meine Routen gelten als wenig sicher und abenteuerlich. Dass sie als abenteuerlich betrachtet werden, macht mich ziemlich stolz. Die kurzen Sportklettereien bieten heute nicht mehr die Möglichkeit, einen Haken oder einen Klemmkeil einzusetzen. Ich habe zwar nichts dagegen, dass einige Routen in bestimmten Sektoren für Anfänger sehr gut eingerichtet sind; aber man sollte nicht übertreiben und sich vor allem gegenseitig respektieren. Für jene Alpinisten, die sich noch in grosse Unternehmungen wagen, sollten einige «Risiko»-Routen bewahrt werden; hier können sie sich auf das ausgesetzte Gelände kombinierter alpiner Touren, wo man nicht stürzen darf, vorbereiten.

Natürlich erachte ich das Ersetzen von altem Sicherungsmaterial als normal. Ich finde es aber völlig daneben, wenn an den gleichen Stellen eine Mehrzahl von Sicherungspunkten angebracht werden. Darin sehe ich eine Form von Inkompetenz und vor allem einen Mangel an Respekt gegenüber mutigen Erstbegehern.

The generation gap

During recent years, technical climbing on steep walls has taken its place alongside traditional mountaineering, although they are two quite separate forms of climbing which, I think, cannot be easily reconciled. The popular routes are becoming increasingly equipped with the aid of a top rope, methods which I would associate with climbing schools and would not consider admissible for the great Alpine faces.

When my friends and I began climbing, we opened new routes using the minimum of climbing equipment, conforming to practices which were regarded as ethical. Today I still follow the same principles. Nowadays aid equipment begins at the foot of the great faces, but bolts have replaced fixed ropes and pitons.

My routes have a reputation for being more daring and less secure. That they should be regarded as more adventurous pleases me. In Sports climbing schools the need to use pitons or wedges no longer arises. In some areas, in fixed sectors where beginners are learning their skills, I am not against the routes being heavily equiped with protection; but, out of consideration for others, this tendency should not be overdone.

Certain routes should be allowed to retain their risk for the benefit of climbers who wish to undertake major Alpine climbs on mixed ground which are often very exposed and do not permit any margin of error.

It is perfectly understandable that old aid points should be replaced when they show signs of weakness, but I find it wholly improper that they should be replaced by a whole new network of equipment. I regard this as a form of incompetence, not to mention disrespect for the daring climbers who first opened the route.

Tentative Kurtyka-Loretan sur la Mazeno Ridge au Nanga Parbat (8125 m). Eté 1997.

1997: Versuch am Mazeno-Grat am Nanga Parbat (8125 m) durch Voytek Kurtyka und Erhard Loretan.

Attempt by V. Kurtyka and E. Loretan on the Mazeno ridge of Nanga Parbat (8125 m), Summer 1997.

Une technique avant-gardiste?

En compagnie d'amis, nous essayons actuellement de mettre en pratique quelques théories que nous jugeons élémentaires.

Nous étant penchés sur les multiples expériences accumulées durant toute l'histoire de l'himalayisme, nous en avons déduit que la rapidité constitue un des principaux vecteurs du succès ou de la survie.

Par expérience, on sait que la majorité des accidents d'altitude sont provoqués par des œdèmes cérébraux ou pulmonaires. La cause? Un défaut d'acclimatation ou un séjour trop prolongé en altitude. On a aussi constaté que, même au repos, le corps ne récupère plus. Au contraire, il continue à se dépenser. Raison pour laquelle, plutôt que de brûler inutilement de l'énergie à tenter de dormir, nous avons pris le parti de marcher jour et nuit.

Lors de nos premières expéditions, je me souviens qu'il me paraissait peu raisonnable de vouloir marcher la nuit par des froids glaciaux. Jusqu'au jour où nous avons tenté l'aventure, en 1985 au K2, avec succès. Depuis lors, je suis systématiquement parti en style non-stop. Ainsi en 1986, à l'Everest, avec Jean Troillet: nous avons gravi la face nord en deux jours, aller et retour.

Ce ne sont pas les records de vitesse qui m'intéressent, mais ce style me permet certainement d'augmenter sensiblement mon assurance-vie…

Avantgardistische Methoden?

Zusammen mit Freunden versuche ich, einige Theorien in die Praxis umzusetzen, die wir als elementar betrachten.

Wir haben uns mit der Menge an Erfahrungen, die in der Geschichte des Höhenbergsteigens gemacht wurden, auseinandergesetzt und daraus gefolgert, dass die Schnelligkeit einer der Hauptfaktoren für den Erfolg und das Überleben ist.

Aus Erfahrung weiss man, dass die meisten Unfälle beim Höhenbergsteigen durch Hirn- und Lungenödeme verursacht werden. Diese Krankheiten wiederum sind auf mangelnde Akklimatisation oder auf einen zu langen Aufenthalt in grosser Höhe zurückzuführen. Man hat auch festgestellt, dass sich der Körper – auch während der Rast – nicht mehr erholt, sondern ständig verausgabt. Deshalb haben wir uns entschlossen, Tag und Nacht weiterzusteigen, anstatt beim Versuch zu schlafen überflüssig Energie zu verbrennen.

Ich erinnere mich daran, dass es mir bei meinen ersten Expeditionen nicht sehr sinnvoll vorkam, nachts, bei eisiger Kälte, unterwegs zu sein; bis zu jenem Tag 1985, als wir am K2 mit dieser Taktik erfolgreich waren. Seither bin ich immer zu Nonstop-Besteigungen aufgebrochen. So etwa 1986 am Everest mit Jean Troillet: Wir benötigten für den Auf- und Abstieg über die Nordflanke zwei Tage.

Schnelligkeitsrekorde interessieren mich nicht, aber der schnelle Stil erlaubt es mir zweifelsohne, meine Überlebenschancen deutlich zu erhöhen!

Advanced technique?

My friends and I have been practising certain theories which we believe to be of basic importance.

Based upon a variety of experiences built up during the whole history of Himalayan climbing, we have come to the conclusion that speed is one of the main determining factors involved in success and survival.

Experience has shown that the majority of high-altitude accidents have been brought about by pulmonary or cerebral oedema, in most cases resulting from insufficient acclimatisation, or spending long spells at high levels, the body deteriorates rather than recuperates even when at rest. For these reasons, we prefer to climb continually, night and day, rather than waste vital energy in attempting to get to sleep during the night.

Until I had followed this principle successfully on K2 in 1985, it had seemed unwise, on earlier expeditions, to attempt to climb during the extreme cold of night-time. But since then I have systematically followed a «non-stop» style of ascent. And it was thus that Jean Troillet and I were able to climb the North Face of Everest and descend from the summit in 2 days.

My concern is not to set up a speed record, but to provide myself with a better chance of survival at high altitudes.

Camp de base du Shisha Pangma (8046 m), Tibet.
Basislager auf der tibetischen Seite des Shisha Pangma (8046 m), Tibet.
Chinese Base Camp below Shisha Pangma (8046 m), Tibet.

La vie quotidienne
Alltagsleben
Village life

La vie dans les villages est très simple. Les gens travaillent juste pour manger et se payer le minimum vital.
Ils ne possèdent pas grand-chose, si ce n'est un trésor bien précieux: le temps.

Der Alltag in den Dörfern ist sehr einfach; die Einheimischen arbeiten, damit sie genug zum Leben haben.
Sie besitzen nicht viel, abgesehen von einem sehr wertvollen Gut: der Zeit.

The people live simply. They work sufficiently to provide themselves with food and basic necessities.
They have few possessions, the most precious of which is time.

Nangpai Gosum (7296 m), le but à peine atteint que déjà d'autres montagnes nous narguent.
Nangpai Gosum (7296 m) – kaum am Ziel angekommen, locken schon andere Berge!
Nangpai Gosum (7296 m), we had hardly reached our objective when other mountains offered fresh challenges.

Vue en direction du Népal depuis le sommet du Cho Oyu (8201 m). Octobre 1990.
Blick vom Gipfel des Cho Oyu (8201 m) auf die nepalesische Seite (Oktober 1990).
Looking towards Nepal from the summit of Cho Oyu (8201 m). October 1990.

En regardant ces images...
  Die Frage nach dem «Warum»,...
  Looking at such scenes,...

… **d**oit-on encore se poser la question «pourquoi»?
… **i**st sie angesichts solcher Bilder nicht hinfällig?
… **i**s it really necessary to ask «why»?

L'acclimatation

L'acclimatation représente la phase la plus importante d'une expédition en haute altitude. Il s'agit d'une période de durée variable, de quelques jours à trois semaines selon les individus. Mais pour certains, l'acclimatation est tout simplement impossible.

Il est indispensable de faire halte entre 4000 et 7000 m d'altitude pour permettre au métabolisme de s'adapter au nouvel environnement. Lors de nos expéditions, nous tentons dans la mesure du possible d'aller passer une nuit vers 7000 m. Ainsi la pression psychologique s'en trouve diminuée les jours suivants. Pour ma part, je ne suis pas favorable à une trop longue période d'acclimatation, car les effets d'un séjour prolongé en altitude, même à 4000 m, sont néfastes. Le corps perd de son potentiel et les «batteries» ne peuvent plus se recharger totalement.

Evidemment, il est aujourd'hui possible de s'acclimater dans des caissons hyperbares au niveau de la mer. Les gens étant de plus en plus pressés et ayant peu de temps à disposition, ils peuvent ainsi «se faire un 8000» à bon compte. Il en est même qui se font transporter au camp de base par hélicoptère! Quant à moi, j'estime qu'il n'y a rien de tel qu'une belle marche d'approche, au contact des populations indigènes, pour apprécier toutes les facettes d'une expédition.

Pour mon acclimatation, je préfère encore passer mes week-ends à la montagne ou partager de bons moments avec des amis dans un bar… Patienter des heures dans des caissons à regarder ses collègues dans le blanc des yeux ne peut que tendre l'atmosphère. Le moment venu, il sera déjà assez difficile de les supporter!

Die Akklimatisation

Die wichtigste Phase einer Expedition in grosse Höhe ist jene der Akklimatisation. Dabei handelt es sich um eine Zeit von unterschiedlicher Länge, die von ein paar Tagen bis zu drei Wochen dauern kann – jeder Mensch ist verschieden, und einige können sich nicht an grosse Höhen akklimatisieren.

Es ist unerlässlich, zwischen 4000 und 7000 m Pausen einzuschalten, um dem Körper die Anpassung an die neue Umgebung zu gestatten. Auf unseren Expeditionen versuchen wir im Rahmen des Möglichen, eine Nacht auf 7000 m zu verbringen. So wird der mentale Druck während der nächsten Tage kleiner. Was mich betrifft, so bin ich nicht für eine allzu lange Akklimatisationszeit, denn die Auswirkungen eines längeren Höhenaufenthalts – und sei es nur auf 4000 m – sind schädlich. Der Körper verliert von seinem Potential, und die «Batterien» können nicht mehr ganz aufgeladen werden.

Natürlich kann man sich heute in Unterdruckkammern auf Meereshöhe vorakklimatisieren. Die Leute, die es heute immer eiliger und immer weniger Zeit zur Verfügung haben, kommen damit billig zu einem Achttausender. Es gibt sogar sogenannte «Bergsteiger», die sich per Helikopter ins Basislager transportieren lassen! Dabei geht meiner Meinung nach nichts über einen schönen Anmarsch, bei dem man der einheimischen Bevölkerung begegnet und alle Facetten einer Expedition schätzen lernt.

Ich akklimatisiere mich lieber, indem ich die Wochenenden in den Bergen oder mit meinen Freunden in einer Bar verbringe, anstatt in einer Unterdruckkammer auszuharren und den Gefährten tief in die Augen zu blicken – das weckt nur Spannungen. Es ist schon schwierig genug, sie unterwegs zu ertragen!

Acclimatisation

One of the most important aspects of expeditions to the highest mountains is the ability to acclimatise to altitude. This ability varies greatly from one person to another and could take between 2-3 days and 2-3 weeks. For some, adapting to high-altitude conditions is impossible.

Between the heights of 4000 m – 7000 m a period of rest is essential to allow the body to adapt to the physical and psychological changes that take place. During our expeditions on which major new climbs have been undertaken, an effort has been made to spend at least one night at around 7000 m, a practice which has been found on succeeding days to diminish the effects of the psychological changes. Personally, I do not believe in a lengthy acclimatisation period, because any prolonged stay even above 4000 m could cause ill-effects. A loss of body strength takes place, and complete physical recuperation is simply not possible. Of course, nowadays, it is possible to acclimatize inside a pressure chamber at sea-level, reaching a level of 8000 m in a relatively short time. It is rather like being transported by helicopter to a high base camp. As far as I am concerned, in order to enjoy every aspect of the atmosphere of an expedition, nothing can compare with the enjoyment of the approach march.

I prefer to acclimatise for an expedition by spending my weekends in the mountains, or by joining a few friends in a bar … To spend hours locked inside a decompression chamber sitting idly causes nothing more than physical and mental strain. It makes the real test, when it comes, perhaps harder to face.

La composition du célèbre thé tibétain: thé, sel et beurre rance. Le boire demande une certaine habitude…
Die Zutaten für den berühmten tibetischen Buttertee: Tee, Salz und ranzige Butter – ein gewöhnungsbedürftiges Getränk …
The ingredients added to the preparation of Tibetan tea are tea, salt, and rancid butter. The practise of drinking it has to be acquired

Vous avez dit «stress»?...
 «stress» – noch nie gehört!
Did you say «stress»...

Malgré leurs outils rudimentaires,
ces artisans sont capables de réaliser
de véritables objets d'art en toute quiétude.

Ohne sich aus der Ruhe bringen
zu lassen, schaffen diese Handwerker
mit ihrem einfachen Werkzeug
regelrechte Kunstwerke.

With primitive tools these craftsmen,
working in a completely relaxed atmosphere,
are able to design really artistic products.

Des trottoirs aux arêtes...
«Gehsteige» in luftiger Höhe...
Pathways along a ridge...

Marcher sur une arête effilée requiert une grande concentration, et demande plus ou moins d'énergie selon le niveau de l'alpiniste.
Die Begehung eines scharfen Grates erfordert grosse Konzentration und je nach Können des Alpinisten mehr oder weniger Energie.
Walking along a sharp ridge calls for all the concentration and energy of a mountaineer.

L'alimentation

«Là-haut», il se passe des choses qui défient les règles de la diététique courante. Si la nourriture joue un rôle important dans la vie d'un camp de base, ce n'est plus une préoccupation majeure en altitude. A ce niveau, tout simplement, l'appétit disparaît. Il faut se faire violence pour manger quelque chose, même après plusieurs jours. Nous vivons le même phénomène que l'on ressent avant de passer un examen important. La tension est si forte que les «conduites» sont bloquées.

Avec Jean, nous avons testé de nombreux produits modernes pour finalement nous retourner vers des choses très simples. Actuellement, on se contente de manger une fondue au pied de la paroi, puis seulement quelques «Ovo Sport» pendant l'ascension.

Dans ce registre, comme dans tant d'autres, nous jouons la carte de l'instinct. La teneur énergétique d'un aliment m'indiffère. Pour moi, aussi simple que cela puisse paraître, l'alimentation, c'est d'abord l'affaire des yeux et du goût. A quoi bon emporter des aliments hyperconcentrés et énergétiques s'ils ne passent pas le cap du sac à dos ou de l'œsophage?

Die Ernährung

«Dort oben» ereignen sich Dinge, die den Regeln der modernen Ernährungslehre widersprechen. Während die Ernährung im Basislager eine wichtige Rolle spielt, gilt ihr weiter oben nicht mehr die Hauptsorge. Auf extremer Höhe verschwindet der Appetit ganz einfach. Man muss sich – auch nach mehreren Tagen – zwingen, etwas zu essen. Wir erleben das Gleiche wie ein Prüfling vor einem wichtigen Examen. Die Spannung ist so gross, dass die «Leitungen» blockiert sind.

Jean und ich probierten verschiedene moderne Produkte aus, bevor wir schliesslich zu einer sehr einfachen Ernährung zurückfanden: Heute begnügen wir uns mit einem Fondue vor dem Aufbruch und ein paar «Ovo Sport» unterwegs.

Wie in vielen anderen Bereichen verlassen wir uns auch beim Essen auf unseren Instinkt. Der Nährwert eines Lebensmittels lässt mich gleichgültig. Die Ernährung ist für mich in erster Linie – so einfach es sich anhören mag – eine Sache der Augen und des Geschmacks. Was bringt es, hochkonzentrierte Produkte mitzunehmen, wenn sie dann im Rucksack oder im Hals steckenbleiben?

Food

Normally accepted forms of diet simply do not apply when one is very high up. Whilst food does have an important rôle to play in the life around base camp, it is no longer a major preoccupation at higher levels where, quite simply, the appetite disappears. One has to force oneself to eat even after some days on a low diet. It is a phenomenon rather like the feeling obtained on the eve of an important examination, a tenseness that seems to overshadow everything else.

Jean Troillet and I have tried out a number of specially designed modern products, only to return to the plain well-tried foods. My personal preference is for a meal of fondue (a seasoned dish of melted cheese) at the foot of the climb, and packets of «Ovo Sport» during the ascent.

In this respect, as in several others, the instinct plays an important part. I do not allow the declared energy value of food to influence my choice; I think that the attraction of any food depends primarily upon its appearance and flavour. Why should we carry packets of concentrated high-energy foods which remain stuck in ones rucksack or throat?

La grande révolution de ces 30 dernières années, le piolet ancreur qui permet l'escalade de goulottes de glace extrêmement raides.

Vor beinahe 30 Jahren kamen die ersten modernen Eisgeräte auf den Markt; damit können auch extrem steile Eisrinnen begangen werden.

A major revolution in climbing equipment in the last 30 years is the modern ice-axe which facilitates the ascent of extremely steep ice channels.

Les équilibristes du Baltoro (Pakistan)
Balancekünstler im Baltoro (Pakistan)
The dexterous Baltis (Pakistan)

Mal chaussés, ces acrobates
des hautes altitudes nous surprennent
par leur dextérité et leur endurance.

Trotz ihres schlechten Schuhwerks
beweisen diese «Akrobaten der extremen
Höhe» eine überraschende Gewandtheit
und Ausdauer.

These high altitude porters
of Baltistan, poorly shod, display
a surprising degree of balance
and endurance.

La boisson

En théorie, en haute altitude, il faudrait normalement ingurgiter cinq à six litres de liquide par jour. Imaginez un peu. Pour obtenir un litre d'eau, il faut fondre de la neige pendant une heure. Ce qui signifie que douze heures – 2 personnes x 6 litres x 1 heure – seraient idéalement nécessaires pour préparer les boissons. Ajoutons-y, dans la pratique courante, douze heures de sommeil et alors, le calcul est vite fait: on friserait le surplace! Ceci démontre encore une fois qu'entre la théorie et la pratique, il y a de la marge…

La relation que l'on entretient à 8000 m avec la boisson est identique à celle que l'on a avec la nourriture. On a rarement soif. D'ailleurs, le goût de l'eau de neige est infect. Personnellement, je n'en consomme que pour une question de survie. Par contre, aussi surprenant que cela puisse paraître, manger de la neige est plus agréable.

Mais qu'on le veuille ou non, il faut bien se forcer à boire pour contrer le risque de gelures. Avec Jean, nous emportons de l'eau depuis le camp de base, en général environ un litre que nous transportons dans une poche de notre veste. Nous y ajoutons un peu de sirop et de la williamine pour éviter qu'elle ne gèle. Nous transportons néanmoins toujours un réchaud dans le sac en cas de coup dur. Quand on pense que pour une ascension de quelque 48 heures on boit à peine un litre, on se demande d'où vient l'énergie.

Encore une fois, il est intéressant de constater que le corps humain est capable de développer cette énergie par la seule force mentale. J'ai l'impression que la tension nerveuse nourrit le corps.

Das Trinken

Auf grosser Höhe sollte man theoretisch fünf bis sechs Liter Flüssigkeit pro Tag zu sich nehmen. Man stelle sich vor: um einen Liter Wasser zu erhalten, muss man eine Stunde lang Schnee schmelzen. Das heisst, dass man zwölf Stunden – zwei Personen mal sechs Liter mal eine Stunde – Zeit haben sollte, um genug Flüssigkeit bereitzustellen. Wenn wir noch zwölf Stunden Schlaf dazugeben, ist die Rechnung schnell gemacht: Man bleibt an der gleichen Stelle stehen – ein weiterer Beweis dafür, dass Theorie und Praxis auseinanderklaffen!

Mit dem Trinken verhält es sich auf 8000 m gleich wie mit dem Essen: Man hat selten Durst. Zudem hat Schneewasser einen widerlichen Geschmack. Ich trinke davon nur, um zu überleben. So überraschend es tönen mag – viel lieber esse ich den Schnee.

Ob man will oder nicht, man muss sich zum Trinken zwingen, um das Risiko von Erfrierungen zu verkleinern. Jean und ich nehmen vom Basislager in einer Jackentasche eine Flasche mit ungefähr einem Liter Wasser mit. Wir fügen ihm etwas Sirup und Williams-Schnaps bei, um sein Gefrieren zu verhindern. Zudem haben wir für Notfälle einen Kocher dabei. Wenn man bedenkt, dass wir bei einer Besteigung von rund 48 Stunden je einen knappen Liter trinken, fragt man sich, woher wir unsere Energie nehmen.

Interessanterweise ist es auch in diesem Bereich die mentale Stärke, die es dem Körper erlaubt, genug Energie zu entwickeln. Ich habe den Eindruck, die psychische Spannung ernähre den Körper regelrecht.

Drink

At high altitudes it is assumed, theoretically, that the body requires 5 to 6 litres of liquid per day. Now just work that one out! Given that one hour is required to melt down sufficient snow to provide 1 litre of water, it would take 12 hours to prepare the ideal quantity of liquid required by 2 climbers in one day. Add to that the normal routine of about 12 hours of rest or sleep, and you will soon see that you enter a vicious circle. Which shows that, as always, there is a world of difference between theory and practice.

At 8000 m, the relevance of drink to the climber is identical to that of food. One rarely feels thirsty, and water melted from snow tastes unpleasant. Personally, I drink it only in order to survive. Surprising though it may seem, I find it more agreeable to eat occasional handfuls of snow.

However, in order to guard against frostbite it is essential to force oneself to drink, like it or not. On departing from base, Jean and I generally carry in our jacket pockets a litre each of water, to which is added a touch of syrup and spirits to prevent it from freezing. For emergencies we also carry a small stove. Considering that for an ascent lasting up to 48 hours one hardly consumes more than a litre of liquid, one wonders where the energy springs from.

Once again it becomes obvious that it is almost solely by sheer mental power that the human body is capable of providing the energy required. I have the impression that it is nervous tension which spurs the body on.

Etranges formations glaciaires sur le glacier du Baltoro, Pakistan.

Eigenartige Eisformationen auf dem Baltoro-Gletscher in Pakistan.

Strange formations on the Baltoro glacier, Pakistan.

La motivation

Me référant à mon expérience personnelle, je puis dire que la motivation est au cœur de la réussite. Plus les objectifs à atteindre paraissent vitaux et plus la motivation est grande. A des stades ultimes, la motivation s'insinue entre la réussite et l'échec.

J'ai gardé très présent à l'esprit le souvenir de cette nuit hivernale au Dhaulagiri. Nous avions prévu une ascension non-stop sommet et retour, si bien que nous étions partis sans matériel de bivouac. En débouchant sur l'arête à 7900 m, le vent faisait rage. Sa violence était telle qu'elle menaçait de m'emporter. Je ne suis pas très lourd, certes, mais de là à m'imaginer entrer en collision avec un avion de ligne… La situation devint si précaire que nous décidâmes de nous arrêter pour la nuit. Une nuit éternelle. En position assise, par une température qu'un congélateur aurait de la peine à atteindre, nous attendions le retour du soleil. Le bruit du vent était terrible. Seul nous rassurait le concert donné par le claquement de nos dents. Des sons caractéristiques qui nous prouvaient que nous faisions encore partie du monde des vivants…

Le plus étrange – ah! la force de la motivation! – est que nous sommes repartis au premier rayon du soleil. Sans cesse, il fallait ancrer nos piolets et nous coucher afin de ne pas être emportés. Le plus extraordinaire est que nous sommes quand même parvenus au sommet.

C'est notamment cette expérience qui m'a confirmé que l'être humain, grâce à sa volonté et à sa motivation, est capable de s'adapter aux pires conditions.

Die Motivation

Aus meiner persönlichen Erfahrung weiss ich, dass die Motivation der Kern jedes Erfolgs ist. Je bedeutender die Ziele sind, desto motivierter ist man, sie zu erreichen. In Grenzsituationen spielt die Motivation das Zünglein an der Waage zwischen Erfolg und Misserfolg.

Ich erinnere mich sehr gut an jene Winternacht am Dhaulagiri: Wir wollten in einem Zug zum Gipfel klettern und absteigen und brachen deshalb ohne Biwakmaterial auf. Als wir auf 7900 m auf den Grat ausstiegen, wütete der Wind und trug uns beinahe davon. Zugegeben, ich bin nicht sehr schwer – aber bis zu jenem Moment war mir die Idee nicht gekommen, ich könnte jemals mit einem Linienflugzeug kollidieren! Unsere Situation war so heikel, dass wir uns entschieden, die Nacht an jener Stelle zu verbringen. Eine ewige Nacht… sitzend, bei einer Temperatur, die auch ein Tiefkühler kaum erreicht, warteten wir auf die Rückkehr der Sonne. Das Geräusch des Winds war schrecklich. Einzig das Konzert unserer Zähne, der klappernde Beweis dafür, dass wir noch zu den Lebenden gehörten, beruhigte uns…

Das Seltsamste ereignete sich am nächsten Morgen: Beim ersten Sonnenstrahl brachen wir auf – Richtung Gipfel. An diesem Entscheid gegen den Abstieg lässt sich die Bedeutung der Motivation ermessen. Immer wieder mussten wir unsere Pickel einrammen und in den Schnee liegen, um nicht vom Wind davongetragen zu werden. Und das Aussergewöhnlichste war, dass wir tatsächlich auf den Gipfel gelangten!

Gerade diese Erfahrung hat mir bestätigt, dass der Mensch sich dank seinem Willen und seiner Motivation den widerwärtigsten Bedingungen anpassen kann.

Motivation

Based on my own experience, I would say that motivation is the essence of success. Each individual tries to discover the elements which enable him to advance in life. The more vital it becomes to achieve a set objective, the greater the motivation. In the final stage, it is motivation that sets the balance between success and failure.

I can still sense clearly what we felt on a certain winter's night on Dhaulagiri. We had planned to climb non-stop to the top and back and did not carry any bivouac equipment. On reaching the N.E. ridge at 7900 m we were struck by a fierce wind which threatened to carry us into the air; with my lightweight body I could almost imagine myself colliding with an airliner in the sky … The situation was becoming precarious and we decided that we would have to halt for the night. A night that seemed without end. In a seated position out in the open, with an air temperature that an ice chamber could hardly match, we awaited the sun's return. The howling of the wind was terrible. The collective chattering of our teeth was the only factor which reassured us that we were still a part of the living world.

Strangest of all, and evidence of the strength of our motivation, was our resumption of the climb at the first ray of sun. In spite of the extreme wind and cold, we continued our upward progress. Time and again we had to bend over our anchored ice axes to prevent our being swept away. It seems incredible that we were able, nevertheless, to reach the summit.

It was this particular experience which convinced me that a human being provided with the will and the motivation is capable of adapting to the most extreme conditions.

La moissonneuse-batteuse à bras. Vallée du Lang Tang, Népal.

Im Langtang-Tal (Nepal): Die Ernte wird von Hand gemäht und gedroschen.

Hand-threshing the harvest, Langtang valley, Nepal.

Le vent et le froid...
      Wind und Kälte...
    Wind and cold...

Ces deux composantes imprègnent déjà les images.
Die zwei auf grosser Höhe prägenden Elemente sind schon auf den Bildern spürbar.
These two elements are manifested even in a photograph.

L'art de souffrir

Le mental joue un rôle déterminant dans le succès d'une ascension. Des études ont démontré très clairement que la capacité physique de l'alpiniste ne diffère en rien de celle d'un autre sportif. Ni de surcapacité pulmonaire, ni régime cardiaque spécial. Sa force, plus qu'aucun autre, il la puise dans son mental.

L'alpiniste de haut niveau doit être capable d'endurer d'impressionnantes souffrances physiques. A 8000 m, le manque d'oxygène, le froid, le vent, la fatigue, le manque de sommeil, l'angoisse, la douleur engendrent des épreuves terribles. C'est pourquoi, à la veille de chaque départ, il faut se poser cette question fondamentale: ai-je encore envie de souffrir? Si sincèrement la réponse est positive, on peut alors se préparer psychologiquement. Il faut tenter de visualiser la course, envisager les pires situations et les analyser minutieusement afin d'éviter la surprise qui peut vite amener à la panique, voire à la mort.

Et une fois dans l'action, il faut oublier la douleur physique, il faut accepter de vivre dans des conditions hostiles. Il n'est plus temps de remettre en question sa présence à ce stade. C'est alors que des termes comme ambition, motivation ou survie prennent tout leur sens. Et puis, à tout instant surgit le souvenir de ce bonheur total, celui-là même que l'on recherche à nouveau. Un instant furtif, total, qui n'a pas de prix. Un instant pendant lequel on ne désire rien d'autre que ce que l'on vit.

Die Kunst des Leidens

Die mentale Verfassung des Bergsteigers spielt bei einer Besteigung die entscheidende Rolle. Studien haben sehr klar aufgezeigt, dass sich die körperliche Leistungsfähigkeit eines Alpinisten nicht grundlegend von jener eines anderen Sportlers unterscheidet. Seine Stärke gründet vielmehr auf seiner geistigen Einstellung.

Ein Alpinist von hohem Niveau muss grosse körperliche Leiden erdulden können. Auf 8000 m stellen ihn Sauerstoffmangel, Kälte, Wind, Erschöpfung, Schlafmangel, Angst und Schmerz vor harte Prüfungen. Daher muss man sich am Vorabend des Aufbruchs die grundlegende Frage stellen: Bin ich bereit zu leiden? Nur wenn die Antwort wirklich positiv ist, kann man sich mental auf das Kommende einstellen. Man muss die Tour visualisieren, sich die schlimmsten Situationen vorstellen und sie minutiös analysieren, um eine Überraschung, die zur Panik und damit zum Tod führen könnte, zu vermeiden.

Einmal aufgebrochen, muss man den körperlichen Schmerz vergessen und akzeptieren, dass man sich in einem lebensfeindlichen Umfeld bewegt. Zu diesem Zeitpunkt darf man seine Anwesenheit nicht mehr hinterfragen - Begriffe wie Ehrgeiz, Motivation und Überleben bekommen hier ihren ganzen Sinn. Und in jedem Moment ist die Erinnerung an das vollendete Glücksgefühl präsent, das man auch dieses Mal wieder sucht. Ein flüchtiger Augenblick, der unbezahlbar ist. Ein Augenblick, in dem man sich nichts anderes wünscht, als ihn zu leben.

The art of suffering

It is the mind which plays a decisive role in the success of any ascent. As a result of studies carried out, it has been shown that there is little difference physically between climbers and other sports people, neither in terms of lung capacity nor in the cardiac system. A climber's strength lies, above all, in the ability to draw upon his mental power.

Extreme climbers should normally possess the capacity to endure exceptional physical suffering. Those who go above 8000 m are exposed to terrible ordeals brought about by a number of factors, oxygen-lack, cold, wind, fatigue, lack of sleep, anxiety, pain. Therefore, anyone prior to setting out on such an exploit should seriously ask himself the fundamental question: do I really want to suffer such an ordeal? If the honest answer is affirmative, the mind must begin to prepare itself psychologically, by creating a visual picture of the climb and analysing carefully the potential situations which might arise, in order to avoid unexpected shocks that could lead to panic or even prove fatal.

Once embarked on the project the mind has to be ready to accept hostile conditions and to ignore any physical hardship. By this stage it is too late to entertain doubts as to why one is there. Now is the time when ambition, motivation, and survival take on their real meaning. Then, suddenly, there will be a reallection of total happiness, a feeling to be sought again and again. A secret moment of fulfilment that is beyond price. A moment when one has no other wish than to be where one is.

Grâce à leur technique de portage, les Népalais sont capables de porter durant des journées entières des charges de plus de 100 kilos.

Die nepalesischen Träger können mit ihrer speziellen Technik tagelang Lasten von über 100 Kilo tragen.

With their unusual style Nepalese porters are able to carry loads of 100 kilos during their daily marches.

Attention, danger!

J'ai souvent entendu de la bouche de néophytes que l'alpiniste va consciemment au-devant du danger, voire de la mort et que, dès lors, il est maître de ses choix. En revanche, ce qui les offusque parfois, ce sont les risques inconsidérés qu'il ferait encourir aux sauveteurs.

Je réfute ces reproches. En effet, personne ne contraint un sauveteur à prendre des risques. Le sauvetage, à l'instar de l'alpinisme, permet à ses adeptes de satisfaire un certain goût du risque et à assouvir des pulsions intérieures.

D'ailleurs, des disproportions dans la perception du risque m'interpellent. De nos jours, la mort rencontrée sur un lieu de travail ou, davantage encore, celle provoquée par la route ne suscite plus que des émotions polies. Mais qu'un alpiniste se tue en montagne et alors l'encre se met à couler.

Je souhaite sincèrement à toutes les personnes irritées à l'idée qu'on puisse prendre de tels risques d'avoir un jour la chance de vivre l'expérience d'une ascension. Alors elles prendraient conscience que les situations ne sont jamais totalement désespérées.

Un atout supplémentaire lorsqu'il s'agit de faire front à des hostilités quotidiennes.

Achtung, Gefahr!

Von Nicht-Bergsteigern wird mir oft gesagt, der Alpinist suche ständig die Gefahr sprich den Tod, und er müsse aus diesem Grund die Folgen seiner Wahl selber tragen; schlimm seien hingegen die unbedachten Risiken, denen er potentielle Retter aussetze.

Solche Vorwürfe weise ich zurück. In Wirklichkeit zwingt niemand einen Retter dazu, Risiken einzugehen. Genau gleich wie der Alpinismus erlaubt das Rettungswesen seinen Anhängern, eine gewisse Risikofreude zu befriedigen und einen inneren Trieb zu stillen.

Mich erstaunt hingegen, wie unterschiedlich das Risiko wahrgenommen wird: Der Tod, dem man am Arbeitsplatz oder auf der Strasse begegnet, weckt heute keine grossen Emotionen mehr. Wenn aber ein Alpinist in den Bergen tödlich verunglückt, fliesst die Tinte…

Jenen Menschen, die sich über die Risikobereitschaft der Bergsteiger ärgern, wünsche ich wirklich, dass sie eines Tages selbst eine Besteigung erleben dürfen. Dabei würden sie verstehen, dass es keine völlig ausweglosen Situationen gibt.

Und diese Erkenntnis ist ein grosser Trumpf bei der Bewältigung der alltäglichen Widerwärtigkeiten.

Danger, beware!

I have often heard it said, usually by novices, that the mountaineer sets out knowingly to face danger, or even death, doing so of his own choosing. What is often overlooked, they say, are the uninvited risks that he exposes potential rescuers when engaged in mountain rescue.

I reject these criticisms. Nobody can compel a rescuer to risk his own life. But, like climbing, rescue work provides the expert with an opportunity to satisfy his inclination to face risks, and to develop his inner strength.

Besides, I would question the disproportionate emphasis given to different levels of risk. Nowadays, death in the work-place or on the roads is not normally an object of great concern. But when a climber dies in the mountains, the ink really begins to flow.

There are some who strongly disapprove of the idea that such risks should be taken. I sincerely wish that they could find an opportunity to take part in a mountain ascent. They would begin to understand that no situation is really as desperate as it may seem; and as an added advantage, it would enable team to face squarely up to lifeis daily adversities.

Coucher de soleil sur le Lhotse (8516 m) et l'Everest (8846 m).
Sonnenuntergang über Lhotse (8516 m) und Everest (8846 m).
Sunset colours over Lhotse (8516 m) and Everest (8846 m).

La peur

J'ai conscience que pour beaucoup, je suis quelqu'un que rien n'effraie, un casse-cou ou un fatigué de la vie. Effectivement, j'avoue aimer le risque. Et pourtant! la vie est si belle que, pour rien au monde, je n'ai envie de la mettre gratuitement en jeu. Autant que possible, j'évite les dangers objectifs, comme une paroi exposée aux chutes de glace ou de pierres. Bien que dans mes expéditions je repousse le plus possible les limites du réalisable, je n'ai jamais sciemment dépassé les miennes. Et j'espère bien avoir l'intelligence de ne jamais le faire. En fait, j'ai pour habitude de toujours garder une marge de sécurité.

A chaque fois que je repars en montagne, je suis angoissé, tendu. Je sais que la moindre faute peut s'avérer fatale. Je dois demeurer extrêmement concentré, car je sais trop bien qui, de la montagne ou de moi, a le plus de risque de tomber…

Cette pression psychologique est d'autant plus intense lorsqu'on atteint les 8000 m, car le manque d'oxygène nous rend encore plus vulnérables.

L'angoisse constitue mon assurance-vie. Si un jour ce sentiment d'impuissance et de respect vis-à-vis de la montagne me quitte, c'est que le temps sera venu de changer… de voie.

Die Angst

Für viele bin ich ein Draufgänger, ein Lebensmüder, kurz – jemand, der vor nichts zurückschreckt. Tatsächlich liebe ich das Risiko. Und doch! Das Leben ist so schön, dass ich es für nichts in der Welt willkürlich aufs Spiel setzen würde. So vermeide ich zum Beispiel die objektiven Gefahren – etwa eine Wand, die Eis- oder Steinschlag ausgesetzt ist – so gut wie möglich. Bei meinen Expeditionen schiebe ich die Grenzen des Machbaren zwar so weit wie möglich hinaus, aber meine Grenzen habe ich nie bewusst überschritten. Und ich hoffe, gescheit genug zu sein, es niemals zu tun – gerade deshalb halte ich ja auch immer eine Sicherheitsmarge ein.

Jedesmal, wenn ich in die Berge aufbreche, bin ich voller Angst und Spannung. Ich weiss, dass sich der kleinste Fehler fatal auswirken kann. Ich bin extrem konzentriert – schliesslich bin ich mir sehr wohl bewusst, dass ich abstürzen könnte!

Dieser psychologische Druck ist noch grösser, wenn man auf 8000 m aufsteigt, wo der Sauerstoffmangel uns viel verletzlicher macht.

Die Angst ist meine Lebensversicherung. Wenn mich dieses Gefühl der Ohnmacht und der Achtung vor den Bergen eines Tages verlassen sollte, wäre es Zeit, einen anderen Weg einzuschlagen!

Fear

I believe that I am someone who generally is not easily frightened or alarmed, whether by a broken limb or by physical or mental weariness. To be honest, I have to admit that I am rather fond of taking risks. And yet – I find it so wonderful to be alive that, not for anything would I deliberately go out to seek danger. As far as possible I make it a point to avoid objective dangers such as faces exposed to falling ice or rock. Although my climbs have been pushed to the extremity of justifiable limits, I have never knowingly exceeded my personal limits. And I believe that I am sufficiently experienced never to allow myself to do so. In fact it has been my practice always to maintain a margin of safety.

I always have a feeling of tension and anxiety every time that I depart for an expedition. I feel a sense of anxiety, because I am aware that the smallest error could have a fatal outcome. Total concentration is essential because I know only too well that the risks of an accident are heavily weighted against me.

Because of the fact that oxygen-lack renders the body more vulnerable physically, this psychological pressure is far more intense at altitudes above 8000 m.

But it is this very mental anxiety that assures my survival. If ever I were to lose my respect for the superior power of the mountains, the time will have come to change my way of life.

Dingboche (4000 m), un village de la vallée du Khumbu au pied du Lhotse (8516 m).

Dingboche (4000 m), ein Dorf im Khumbu am Fuss des Lhotse (8516 m).

Dingboche village in the Khumbu valley situated at the foot of Lhotse (8516 m).

Escalade en terrain mixte
  Klettern in kombiniertem Gelände
 Mixed climbing

Il est rare que l'on enlève nos crampons lors de nos ascensions combinées rocher-glace. Le crissement de ceux-ci sur le rocher devient un bruit familier.

Beim Klettern in Fels und Eis ziehen wir unsere Steigeisen nur selten aus; ihr Kratzen und Knirschen auf dem Fels wird zum vertrauten Geräusch.

On combined rock and ice one usually climbs without removing crampons, growing familiar with their grating sound on the rocks.

Durant l'ascension, ce n'est qu'au bivouac que l'on prend vraiment le temps d'admirer le paysage. Nanga Parbat 1997.
Während einer Besteigung kommt man nur im Biwak dazu, die Landschaft richtig zu geniessen. Nanga Parbat, 1997.
During an ascent it is only at a bivouac that one really gets a chance to admire the scenery. Nanga Parbat 1997.

Le moment le plus attendu lors de nos ascensions non-stop, l'arrivée du jour, Mazeno-Ridge. Eté 1997.
Tagesanbruch am Mazeno-Grat (1997) – der Augenblick, den wir bei unseren Nonstop-Besteigungen am sehnlichsten erwarten.

Savoir renoncer

Le renoncement constitue l'une des conditions sine qua non de la survie. Il est difficile d'abandonner à proximité du but. C'est dans ces moments-là que l'expérience pèse de tout son poids.

Lorsqu'on se trouve à quelques encablures du sommet, la tentation est grande de prendre un surcroît de risques. Le fait de savoir qu'on ne pourra pas tenter une nouvelle fois l'ascension dans un délai rapproché, l'orgueil, la fierté, l'argent et le temps engagés influencent souvent l'alpiniste dans ses choix.

Il est indispensable d'ancrer certains paramètres très fort dans son cerveau afin que, le moment venu, on fasse pencher la balance du côté de la sagesse. Je me suis toujours persuadé qu'il ne vaut pas la peine de sacrifier ne serait-ce qu'un bout de doigt pour accéder à un sommet.

Il faut oser écouter et faire confiance à son instinct.

Verzichten können

Verzichten können – das ist eine der unerlässlichen Bedingungen, will man in den Bergen überleben. Es ist schwierig, in der Nähe des Ziels aufzugeben. In diesen Augenblicken ist die eigene Erfahrung unbezahlbar.

Befindet man sich ein paar Seillängen vor dem Gipfel, ist die Versuchung gross, zu hohe Risiken einzugehen. Das Wissen, dass man die Besteigung nicht gleich ein weiteres Mal versuchen kann, der Stolz, das Geld und die Zeit, die eine solche Expedition kosten, beeinflussen den Bergsteiger oft in seinen Entscheidungen.

Man muss ein paar Parameter sehr fest im Kopf verankern, damit die Waage im entscheidenden Moment in die richtige Richtung – jene der Besonnenheit und Vernunft – ausschlägt. Es war immer meine Überzeugung, dass ein Gipfel nicht den Verlust einer Fingerspitze wert ist.

Man muss es wagen, dem inneren Gefühl – dem Instinkt – zu folgen und zu vertrauen.

Knowing when to stop

To turn back in time constitutes one of the most vital conditions for survival. When the goal appears to be so near it is very difficult to decide to give up the struggle. This is the critical point at which the weight of experience really counts.

Upon reaching a point a few rope-lengths from the summit, the temptation to overstep the margin of risk is enormous. There are usually several factors which trouble the choice that the climber must make: the knowledge that a second chance will not be soon available, greed, pride, money and the time involved.

It is imperative to fix firmly in the brain certain parameters, which could at the critical moment direct the mind towards a wise decision. I have always believed strongly that no summit is worth the sacrifice of even the tips of my fingers.

One must dare to have confidence in one's instincts and to listen to them.

Quatorze jours d'effort pour tracer un nouvel itinéraire dans cette fabuleuse tour du Trango (6257 m). Eté 1988, Kurtyka-Loretan

Sommer 1988: Voytek Kurtyka und Erhard Loretan benötigen 14 Tage, um eine Neutour an den fantastischen Nameless Tower (6257 m, Trango-Gebiet) zu legen.

Fourteen days of struggle to open a new route on this fabulous 6257 m tower, Trango Group, Summer 1988, Kurtyka-Loretan

Un rêve se réalise…
　　Ein Traum wird wahr…
　　A dream comes true…

Le rêve de chaque himalayiste: poser son pied sur le toit du monde.
Cette chance, je l'ai eue avec Jean Troillet en été 1986 en escaladant la face nord directe de l'Everest.

Jeder Höhenbergsteiger träumt davon, das Dach der Welt zu betreten;
dies gelang mir 1986, als ich mit Jean Troillet die Everest-Nordflanke durchstieg.

Every himalayan climber dreams of stepping onto the roof of the world. I had the opportunity
to do so in the summer of 1986 with Jean Troillet when we climbed the North face of Everest.

La photographie

Réaliser des photographies en montagne n'est pas chose aisée. Il y a évidemment la photo facile d'un paysage prise durant la marche d'approche. Photographier les indigènes dans leurs activités quotidiennes est déjà plus ardu. Dans ces situations, j'avoue ressentir une certaine gêne, car il faut pratiquement «voler» le sujet pour assurer un effet authentique. La photo d'action en montagne est une toute autre affaire. Le froid met le matériel à rude épreuve. Et puis il faut véritablement se forcer pour sortir la camera dans certaines situations. Afin d'assurer de futurs projets, il est pourtant important de rapporter des documents visuels.

Je me souviens d'une photo qui a bien failli me coûter quelques doigts. C'était durant l'ascension hivernale du Dhaulagiri (8167 m) en compagnie de Pierre-Alain Steiner et Jean Troillet. Le soleil avait disparu, le froid se faisait de plus en plus vif. Nous nous trouvions à une altitude d'environ 7900 m. Nous avions l'impression d'évoluer dans une soufflerie et nous nous préparions à affronter la pire nuit de notre existence. Nous ne disposions pas de matériel de bivouac. En vain, nous cherchions une possibilité de creuser un trou pour nous abriter du vent. Il fallait absolument que j'immortalise ces instants un peu surréalistes. Avec peine, je sortis mon appareil de la veste. Et pour effectuer les réglages, je dégageai mes mains de mes gants en duvet. Cela ne dura que quelques secondes, mais déjà deux de mes doigts étaient blancs.

Je réussis à les sauver au prix d'énormes douleurs: je les frappai pendant de longues minutes avec mon marteau…

Fotografieren unterwegs

Das Fotografieren in den Bergen ist nicht leicht. Natürlich gibt es die einfachen Landschaftsbilder, die man auf dem Anmarsch schiesst. Schwieriger ist es schon, die Einheimischen bei ihrer täglichen Arbeit im Bild festzuhalten. Ich empfinde dabei gewisse Hemmungen, da man das Sujet «stehlen» muss, um Authentizität zu erzielen. Ganz was anderes ist die «Action»-Fotografie an den hohen Bergen: Die Kälte unterzieht das Material einer harten Prüfung. Und zudem muss man sich wirklich zwingen, die Kamera in gewissen Situationen überhaupt hervorzunehmen. Um weitere Projekte zu sichern, ist es allerdings wichtig, dass man mit Aufnahmen von einer Expedition zurückkommt.

Ich erinnere mich an ein Bild, das ich während der Winterbesteigung des Dhaulagiri (8167 m) zusammen mit Pierre-Alain Steiner und Jean Troillet aufnahm und das mich beinahe ein paar Finger gekostet hätte: Die Sonne war untergegangen, die Kälte wurde immer bissiger. Wir befanden uns auf rund 7900 m und hatten den Eindruck, in eine Windmaschine geraten zu sein und uns auf die schlimmste Nacht unseres Lebens vorbereiten zu müssen. Biwakmaterial hatten wir keines dabei. Vergeblich versuchten wir, ein Loch zu schaufeln, um uns vor dem Wind zu schützen. Ich musste diese etwas surreal anmutenden Augenblicke unbedingt festhalten: Mühevoll zog ich meinen Fotoapparat aus der Tasche und zog meine Daunenhandschuhe aus, um die paar Handgriffe vorzunehmen. Diese Handlung dauerte nur ein paar Sekunden, aber zwei meiner Finger waren danach weiss!

Es gelang mir, sie auf äusserst schmerzvolle Art zu retten: Ich bearbeitete sie minutenlang mit meinem Kletterhammer …

Photography

Mountain photography can be difficult. Although it may be fairly easy on the approach march to capture the atmosphere of the countryside, what I have found particularly hard is to try to capture scenes of the local people engaged in their daily activities. To obtain an authentic effect one needs to be very quick to seize exactly the right opportunity. It is altogether different with action photographs on the mountain, particularly under extreme conditions, when the equipment is affected by excessive cold; and there are times when a real effort has to be made merely to draw the camera out in order to provide a visual record and to obtain a useful reference for planning some future project.

One photograph I can never forget because I narrowly escaped frostbitten fingers. It was taken during my winter ascent of Dhaulagiri 8167 m with Pierre-Alain Steiner and Jean Troillet. We were at a height of about 7900 m; the sun had disappeared, and the cold was gradually becoming more intense. We had the impression that we were trapped in a wind-tunnel, and, without any bivouac equipment, we were expecting to face one of the coldest nights of our lives. We tried in vain to dig a hole that would protect us from the worst of the wind. Desperately anxious to capture a glimpse of this surrealistic scene I extracted my camera from my inner pocket, and, in order to set the exposure, I removed my outer duvet gloves. This took no more than a few seonds, but I noticed that two of my fingers had turned white. Beating them with my climbing hammer for several minutes afterwards, accompanied by excruciating pain, I was able to save them.

Le danger le plus redoutable: le sérac qui peut se détacher à n'importe quel moment du jour ou de la nuit.

Die bedrohlichste Gefahr: Eistürme, die jederzeit, tags und nachts, abbrechen können.

The most terrifying danger: a serac which could crash down at any moment, day or night.

La zone de la mort

La zone de la mort? C'est selon moi une partie du monde entre le ciel et la terre, où tout est différent.

A partir d'une certaine altitude, la diminution très importante d'oxygène a des effets extrêmement sensibles sur l'organisme. Pour s'adapter à ce nouvel environnement, les globules rouges se multiplient considérablement, rendant le sang plus épais. Ils permettent de véhiculer plus d'oxygène, mais les effets peuvent se révéler très néfastes.

L'irrigation des extrémités devient difficile, le risque de gelure est alors énorme. Les gestes deviennent lourds, le cerveau perd de ses aptitudes, les réflexes fléchissent. A ce stade critique, l'alpiniste se trouve réellement en danger de mort. Une mauvaise décision, une heure de trop passée en altitude… et voilà l'éternité qui se profile!

Les gens «d'en bas», qui veulent toujours tout comprendre, tentent d'analyser, de déceler l'erreur, et surtout de désigner le responsable d'un drame. Je sais par expérience qu'on ne peut pas porter de jugement sur ce qui s'est passé dans cette zone dite «de la mort». On peut tout au plus dénoncer le style d'une expédition, les moyens techniques mis en œuvre ou tout simplement l'incompétence.

«Là-haut», l'être humain prend des décisions qu'il ne prendrait pas forcément à 4000 m. Le geste devient instinctif. Le choix peut garantir la survie; mais il peut aussi conduire à la mort.

Die Todeszone

Die Todeszone? Sie ist für mich eine Gegend zwischen Himmel und Erde, wo alles anders ist.

Von einer gewissen Höhe an hat der geringere Sauerstoffdruck der Luft extreme Auswirkungen auf den Körper. Um sich an die neue Umgebung anzupassen, nehmen die roten Blutkörperchen beträchtlich zu und verdicken das Blut. Sie erlauben den Transport von mehr Sauerstoff, doch die Folgen können sehr schädlich sein.

Die Durchblutung der Glieder ist viel schlechter und das Risiko von Erfrierungen sehr hoch. Die Bewegungen werden schwerfällig, das Gehirn verliert Fähigkeiten, die Reflexe werden langsamer. In diesem kritischen Stadium befindet sich der Alpinist tatsächlich in Todesgefahr. Eine falsche Entscheidung, eine Stunde zu lang in grosser Höhe – und der Tod rückt in die Nähe.

Die Menschen, die sich in den «Niederungen» aufhalten und immer alles verstehen möchten, versuchen, zu analysieren, den Fehler zu suchen und vor allem – bei einem Drama – einen Verantwortlichen zu nennen. Ich weiss aus Erfahrung, dass man sich über Ereignisse, die sich in der Todeszone abspielen, kein Urteil bilden kann. Man kann höchstens den Stil einer Expedition kritisieren, ihre technischen Mittel oder die mangelnde Kompetenz.

«Dort oben» fasst der Mensch Entschlüsse, die er auf 4000 m nicht unbedingt fassen würde. Er handelt instinktiv. Ein einziger Entscheid kann das Überleben sichern, doch er kann auch zum Tod führen.

The death zone

The death zone? I regard this as a region apart, situated between the earth and the sky, where everything is different.

Above a certain height the greatly reduced oxygen in the atmosphere generates perceptible reactions in the human organism. The body adjusts to the new situation by means of a considerable increase in the red blood-cell count, which results in thickening of the blood, allowing oxygen to flow more freely through the veins; but these changes bring about undesirable effects.

The flow of blood to the extremities of the body is much diminished, making those areas extremely vulnerable to frostbite. There is a slowing down in movement, a reduction in brain function, and a weakening of the reflexes. A climber who arrives at this stage is in serious danger of death. A false decision, or an hour longer spent at this level, and he is heading for eternity.

Valley dwellers who like to think that they can find reasons for everything will analyse, point out errors, and announce the cause of the climbing disaster. I know from experience that it is unwise to pretend that one can judge precisely what may have happened in the so-called «death-zone». At the most, one might criticize the style of the expedition, its general set-up, or merely its sheer incompetence.

At high altitudes the human being makes decisions which he would not necessarily make at 4000 m. He acts instinctively. His action could lead to his survival; it could also bring about his death.

Porteurs baltis sur le glacier du Baltoro. En toile de fond, le Muztagh Tower (7273 m, Pakistan).

Balti-Träger auf dem Baltoro-Gletscher – im Hintergrund der Muztagh Tower (7273 m, Pakistan).

Balti porters on the Baltoro glacier, with the Muztagh Tower (7273 m) in the background.

Belle lumière
     Magisches Licht
  Marvellous radiance

La beauté de ces montagnes vaut bien quelques souffrances…
Die Schönheit der Berge ist die Leiden wert…
It is worthwhile suffering a little in order to experience the beauty of the mountains…

Les passages
Beschwerliche Passagen
Making his way

Le parcours du porteur est semé d'obstacles en tous genres. Si le porteur veut gagner son salaire,
il est obligé d'être polyvalent et de passer partout; mais dans la difficulté tout le monde est solidaire.

Der Weg des Trägers ist von Hindernissen aller Art gesäumt; will er seinen Lohn erhalten,
muss er sie überwinden und dabei vielseitig sein – und bei schwierigen Stellen helfen alle einander.

The porter's path is strewn with all kinds of difficulties. If he wants to earn his wage he must be ready
to do anything that is required. But he can count on the support of his colleagues in case of trouble.

L'escalade de nuit
   Nachts unterwegs
 Night-climbing

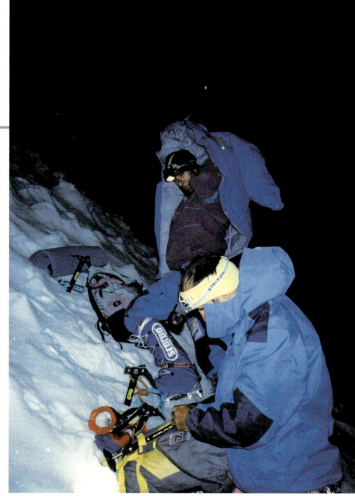

Afin d'augmenter nos chances de réussite et de survie, nous tentons de gravir les sommets dans un style non-stop.
Wir versuchen, unsere Erfolgs- und Überlebenschancen zu erhöhen, indem wir die Gipfel nonstop besteigen.
To increase our chances of success and survival we have adopted a «non-stop» style.

La nuit approche, la tension nerveuse est à son comble. Dans quelques instants, ce sera le départ pour le Lhotse.
Die Nacht bricht an, die Spannung erreicht den Höhepunkt: in wenigen Augenblicken brechen wir zum Lhotse auf.
As night approaches, nervous tension begins to rise. Our ascent of Lhotse is about to begin.

L'état de la neige décide de la réussite ou de l'échec d'une expédition.
Die Schneeverhältnisse entscheiden oft über den Erfolg oder das Scheitern einer Expedition.
Snow conditions dictate the success or failure of the venture.

Les gens
  Die Menschen
The local people

Ils connaissent encore les vraies valeurs de la vie et n'ont pas besoin d'artifice pour se mettre en valeur.
Ils sont beaux et purs, tout simplement.

Sie kennen noch die wahren Werte des Lebens und brauchen keine Tricks, um sich zur Geltung zu bringen;
in ihrer Einfachheit sind sie schön und rein.

They recognise the real values of life and have no need to try to add to them by artificial means.
Their lives are noble and pure.

La marche d'approche
Auf dem Anmarsch
The approach march

Engager une colonne de porteurs amène quotidiennement son lot de problèmes. Pour nous aussi le moment de leur prière signifie un moment de répit.

Wer eine ganze Kolonne von Trägern beschäftigt, muss jeden Tag mit ein paar Problemen rechnen – ausser zu den Gebetszeiten der Träger!

Hiring a group of porters brings about a quota of daily problems. Their prayer halt provides us with a few moments of relaxation.

Seul maître à bord

Dans certaines circonstances, je m'interroge: jusqu'à quel point suis-je seul maître à bord? En altitude, le sentiment d'impuissance face à une nature qui peut se révéler hostile est fréquent. Dans ces moments de doute ou de crise, on s'imagine à quel point on ne représente qu'une molécule dans l'univers. A dire vrai, j'ai souvent eu l'impression d'être guidé par une force extérieure.

Il y a certains risques que j'ai pris parce que je sentais que j'en avais la permission et qu'il ne m'arriverait rien. En haute altitude, la notion de danger n'a plus le même sens que sur le plancher des vaches.

En 1986, à l'Everest, avec Jean Troillet, les conditions durant l'ascension étaient si difficiles que, sans une force extérieure qui nous animait, seuls avec notre corps, nous n'aurions pas réussi. Nous avons traversé des pentes de neige extrêmement profondes, qui pouvaient à tout moment se détacher. J'ai le sentiment qu'à 4000 m, nous ne les aurions pas franchies, mais là, je me sentais protégé. J'avais l'impression que je devais aller jusqu'au bout afin de pouvoir vivre une expérience très importante de ma vie: ou savourer les délices d'une présence au sommet de la Terre ou m'en aller dans un autre monde.

Herr der Lage?

Manchmal frage ich mich, wie weit ich auf grosser Höhe wirklich Herr meiner Entscheide bin. Dort oben empfindet man oft ein Gefühl der Ohnmacht gegenüber der Natur, die sich feindlich zeigen kann. In diesen Augenblicken des Zweifels oder der Krise wird man sich bewusst, dass man wirklich nur ein Molekül in einem unendlichen Universum ist – und in solchen Augenblicken habe ich, ehrlich gesagt, oft das Gefühl gehabt, von einer äusseren Kraft geleitet zu werden.

So konnte ich gewisse Risiken eingehen, weil ich mich dazu berechtigt fühlte und spürte, dass mir nichts zustossen würde. In grosser Höhe hat der Begriff Gefahr nicht mehr den gleichen Sinn wie auf dem «festen Boden».

Als ich 1986 zusammen mit Jean Troillet am Everest unterwegs war, waren die Verhältnisse während der Besteigung so schwierig, dass wir den Gipfel allein mit unseren Körpern, ohne eine äussere Kraft, die uns antrieb, nicht geschafft hätten. Wir spurten Tiefschneehänge, die jeden Moment als Lawine hätten abgehen können. Ich glaube, auf 4000 m hätten wir uns nicht in solche Flanken gewagt, aber dort fühlte ich mich geschützt. Ich hatte den Eindruck, ich müsse bis zum Letzten gehen, um eine für mein Leben sehr wichtige Erfahrung zu machen: Entweder die Wonne, auf dem höchsten Gipfel der Erde zu stehen oder dann das Erlebnis, in eine andere Welt überzugehen.

In sole charge

Under certain conditions I have sometimes asked myself: up to what point do I remain in full control? At high altitudes there are frequent occasions when one feels powerless against hostile natural forces. At such moments of crisis or self-doubt, a point is reached when one sees oneself as a tiny molecule in a vast universe. In truth, there have been times when I have had the impression of being guided by an external force.

When you are high up in the mountains the notion of danger does not have the same significance as on terra firma. Sometimes I have taken risks guided by the feeling of having had permission to do so without danger of coming to any harm.

On the North Face of Everest in 1986, Jean Troillet and I found the conditions terribly difficult; our bodies alone, without the aid of some external force, would not have succeeded. We were traversing slopes of extremely deep snow which could have avalanched at any moment. I believe that if we were at 4000 m in the Alps we would not have continued; but up there I somehow had a feeling that we were protected. I felt intensely that I had to complete the ascent in order to gain an experience of great personal importance: to relish the happiness of standing on the summit of the earth, or to take a step into another world.

Sortant de la brume, ce pic dévoile quelques-uns de ses mystères…
Der aus dem Nebel aufragende Gipfel enthüllt einige seiner Geheimnisse …
Coming out of the clouds, this peak reveals some of its mysteries …

Le sponsoring

Le sponsoring est un métier difficile. Il faut être à la fois bon vendeur et ne pas avoir trop de scrupules. En un mot, l'antithèse de ce qu'est ma nature, si bien que je n'ai jamais décroché de contrats mirobolants.

Mes premières expéditions étaient en partie financées par les gens de la région, que je remercie encore. Avec mes copains d'expédition, nous vendions des cartes postales, des tee-shirts ou encore des bouteilles de vin. Les livraisons, quelle aventure! Les destinataires étant généralement des amis, on ne rentrait pas toujours de sang-froid à la maison…

En 1985, une rencontre fortuite m'a mis en contact avec un homme extraordinaire, le D' Rodolphe Zingg, «Don Rodolpho», un pionnier de la recherche de marchés en Suisse et fondateur de la maison IHA à Hergiswil, dont le rayonnement devint vite international. Il entreprit spontanément de me soutenir. Mais hélas! ses démarches auprès de sponsors potentiels demeurèrent sans succès. C'est alors que lui vint l'idée de fonder le club «8000 E. Loretan». C'est grâce à celui-ci qu'une bonne partie de mes rêves devint réalité. Ruedi Zingg avait immédiatement deviné que ma liberté n'a pas de prix. Son club me permit de partir chaque fois sans subir de pressions, l'esprit libre.

Aujourd'hui, je vole de mes propres ailes. Néanmoins, le club «8000 E. Loretan» continue à exister. L'argent récolté sert d'autres causes humanitaires. Entre autres opérations, nous organisons chaque année des camps gratuits pour des jeunes en difficulté.

Sponsoring

Das Sponsoring ist eine schwierige Branche: Man muss sich einerseits gut verkaufen können, anderseits nicht zu grosse Skrupel haben. Kurz gesagt – Voraussetzungen, die meinem Charakter genau entgegenlaufen! Deshalb habe ich auch nie grossartige Sponsorverträge geangelt.

Meine ersten Expeditionen wurden teilweise durch Leute aus der Region finanziert – ich bin ihnen heute noch zu Dank verpflichtet. Zusammen mit meinen Expeditionskollegen verkaufte ich ihnen Postkarten, T-Shirts oder Wein … Die Lieferung der Weinflaschen war jeweils ein Abenteuer! Die Empfänger waren normalerweise Freunde, und wir kehrten nicht immer mit einem klaren Kopf nach Hause zurück.

1985 begegnete ich zufällig einem aussergewöhnlichen Mann: Dr. Rodolphe (Ruedi) Zingg, «Don Rodolpho» genannt, seines Zeichens Pionier auf dem Gebiet der Marktforschung in der Schweiz und Gründer der IHA in Hergiswil, die bald international tätig war. Spontan begann er, mich zu unterstützen. Seine Bemühungen bei möglichen Sponsoren blieben aber leider erfolglos. Darauf hatte er die Idee, den Klub «8000 E. Loretan» zu gründen. Dank dieser Vereinigung wurden zahlreiche meiner Träume Wirklichkeit. Ruedi Zingg erkannte sofort, dass meine Freiheit unbezahlbar war. Der von ihm initiierte Klub erlaubte es mir, auf jede Expedition ohne Druck, mit freiem Geist aufzubrechen.

Heute bin ich flügge. Den Klub «8000 E. Loretan» gibt es zwar immer noch. Das gesammelte Geld dient aber anderen, humanitären Zwecken: So organisieren wir unter anderem jedes Jahr kostenlose Lager für Jugendliche aus schwierigen Verhältnissen.

Sponsoring

This is an art difficult to master. One has got to be a terrific talker and a skilful salesman, prepared also to swallow one's scruples. In a word one requires all the qualities against which my nature utterly rebels; and I have never succeeded in pulling off some marvellous contract.

My earliest expeditions were supported financially by people from the region around where I live and I cannot thank them enough for their kindness. With a group of friends who made up our expedition, we sold postcards, tee-shirts, and bottles of wine bearing special labels. Delivery was an amusing adventure! Since most of the receivers were friends, the evenings were usually prolonged, and our course homeward tended to be a bit unsteady …

In 1985, I had a chance encounter with a remarkable person Dr. Rodolphe Zingg, 'Don Rodolpho', a pioneer of Market Research in Switzerland and founder of the Company I.H.A. in Hergiswil, with interests extending worldwide. He voluntarily undertook to support me; but alas, his efforts to find suitable sponsors were unsuccessful. He decided then to found a «Club 8000 E. Loretan». It is thanks to him that I have been able to turn a large part of my dreams into reality. Ruedi Zingg was quick to perceive that I regarded my personal freedom as beyond price. The Club that he founded enabled me to set out on every new venture free from any pressures or obligations.

Today, although I am self-supporting, the «Club 8000 E. Loretan» continues to exist. Its accumulated funds now serve humanitarian causes, amongst which are the organising free camping holidays for young people of limited means.

Pour l'alpiniste qui recherche les nouveautés, l'Himalaya offre encore d'énormes possibilités. Népal.

Dem Bergsteiger auf der Suche nach Neuland bietet der Himalaya – wie hier in Nepal – unzählige Möglichkeiten.

For the climber looking for new experiences, the Himalaya offers immense possibilities. Nepal.

Au bout de l'effort, l'apothéose...
  Nach der Anstrengung die Krönung...
  Moment of glory at the end of the struggle...

Lorsque l'on atteint le sommet, il y a quelques secondes où nous goûtons au bonheur total.
Auf dem Gipfel geniessen wir ein paar Sekunden lang das vollständige Glücksgefühl.
On reaching the summit, there is a brief moment of total happiness.

La cordée

Aujourd'hui, le terme de cordée est remis en question. L'activité en montagne a pris une tournure plus individualiste, à l'instar de notre société.

Les ascensions en solitaire sont à la mode, pourtant le mot «cordée» garde toujours la même signification. Certes, le temps des grandes cordées héroïques est passé. La corde n'en constitue plus le symbole. En quelque sorte, elle est remplacée par le feeling et le vécu de deux grimpeurs, unis par une même éthique et capables de se comprendre dans la sobriété des mots. Le symbole de la corde qui sauve, aussi, s'est atténué. On a pris conscience que cette corde est à l'alpinisme ce que la ceinture de sécurité est à la voiture. Elle peut sauver, certes, mais elle peut aussi tuer. Dans certaines situations, elle peut entraîner la mort de deux personnes au lieu d'une…

En Himalaya, il est rare qu'on progresse encordé. A de telles altitudes, chacun adopte son propre rythme de marche… Dès lors, la corde contrarierait une progression naturelle. Du fait du manque d'oxygène, les réflexes diminuent. Afin d'enrayer une chute, il faut être soit très rapide, soit assuré à un point fixé dans la glace ou le rocher, ce qui se pratique rarement à haute altitude.

Dans la relation qu'entretiennent le guide et son client, la situation se présente différemment. La notion de responsabilité impose l'utilisation de la corde car, généralement, le client s'en remet entièrement entre les mains de son guide… par la corde qui les relie.

Die Seilschaft

Der Begriff Seilschaft ist heute in Frage gestellt. Das Bergsteigen hat – als Abbild unserer Gesellschaft – einen individualistischeren Zug angenommen.

Alleingänge sind «in», doch das Wort Seilschaft hat immer noch die gleiche Bedeutung, obwohl die Zeiten der grossen, heroischen Seilschaften vorbei sind. Das Seil verkörpert nicht mehr das gleiche Symbol. Es wird gewissermassen durch das Gefühl und die Erfahrung von zwei Kletterern, die die gleiche Ethik verbindet und die sich in nüchternen Worten verstehen, ersetzt. Auch das Symbol des rettenden Seils ist nicht mehr so stark. Man ist sich bewusst geworden, dass das Bergseil den Sicherheitsgurten im Auto entspricht: Es kann natürlich eine rettende Funktion haben, es kann aber auch umbringen. In gewissen Situationen kann es den Tod von zwei miteinander verbundenen Menschen verursachen.

Im Himalaya klettert man nur selten am Seil: Auf grosser Höhe nimmt jeder sein eigenes Tempo an. Das Seil würde den natürlichen Rhythmus nur hemmen. Die Reflexe werden durch den Sauerstoffmangel verlangsamt; um einen Sturz aufzuhalten, müsste man entweder sehr schnell sein oder sich an einem Punkt im Eis oder im Fels sichern, was wiederum auf grosser Höhe nur selten der Fall ist.

Bei der Beziehung zwischen einem Bergführer und seinem Gast verhält es sich anders: Die Verantwortung des Bergführers setzt den Gebrauch des Seils voraus, denn normalerweise vertraut der Gast sein Leben den Händen des Bergführers an – in Form des Seils, das sie verbindet.

The rope team

Opinions are divided about the effectiveness of roped climbing. In common with changes in modern society, mountaineering has adopted a more independent direction.

Solitary climbing is now considered fashionable. Yet the security of a roped climb still retains its special significance. Certainly, the heroic days of famous rope-teams is past. The rope has little more than a symbolic value. It provides, instead, a sense of unity between two climbers who share the same ethical values and have achieved a close understanding which requires few words. The symbol of safety which the rope provides is limited. The climber regards the rope with a feeling of security similar to that of a car-driver wearing a safety-belt; it could save just as easily as it could kill. In certain situations the use of the climbing rope could result in two deaths instead of one.

Roped ascents are now becoming rare in the Himalaya. Since high-altitude climbers adopt their individual pace, the use of the rope would interfere with the natural rhythm of each. Lack of oxygen reduces the sharpness of physical reflexes. To prevent a fall one must either act very swiftly, or else set up fixed belay points in the ice or rock, a practice not often adopted at very high altitudes.

The situation in a guide-client relationship is quite different. The guide is responsible for the client's safety, which imposes the need for a rope since, as is often the case, the client relies heavily upon the skills of his guide by means of the rope which unites them.

Ces nomades des hauts plateaux tibétains sont démunis; leur richesse: la beauté des cimes.

Die Nomaden der tibetischen Hochebenen sind arm – aber bereichert durch die Schönheit der Gebirgslandschaft.

These nomads of the lofty Tibetan plateau possess, if nothing else, the capacity to contemplate the beauty of these mountains.

Les transports

Transportmöglichkeiten

Forms of transport

Les moyens de se déplacer de la plaine au camp de base sont très variés.
Le plus sûr reste néanmoins celui qui se déplace sur des «pattes».

Es gibt verschiedene Möglichkeiten, um vom Tiefland ins Basislager zu gelangen –
am sichersten ist, wer sich auf «vier Beinen» dorthin bewegt.

Various means of transport are required to reach base camp.
The most reliable is the four-legged variety.

L'esprit d'équipe

Le choix du partenaire n'est pas toujours facile, surtout pour des expéditions de plusieurs mois.

Cela peut paraître paradoxal, mais bien que l'on se retrouve dans l'immensité d'une nature sauvage, le camp de base paraît vite exigu. Les tensions augmentent de jour en jour et la cohabitation devient de plus en plus difficile. Et plus le nombre de coéquipiers est élevé, plus le problème s'affirme. C'est notamment pour cette raison qu'aujourd'hui je ne pars plus qu'en toute petite équipe.

La cordée Troillet-Loretan est sans nul doute en Himalaya le tandem qui a duré le plus longtemps. Il n'y a pas de recette miracle, juste quelques règles simples à respecter.

Le silence parfois angoissant du camp de base n'est guère troublé par de longues conversations. Jean et moi sommes très différents. On ne cherche même pas à mieux se connaître, notre vécu suffit. L'alpiniste étant plutôt introverti, il nous arrive souvent de ne pas causer durant plusieurs jours. Nous réussissons à gérer une certaine tension, parce que dans l'action nous sommes comme deux machines parfaitement au diapason. Le jour «J», nos échanges de paroles se font encore plus rares, car les théories ne donnent jamais des ailes…

Avec Jean, je partage la même conception de la montagne, nos motivations et nos convictions sur les stratégies à adopter sont identiques. Ce sont là les recettes de notre long compagnonnage.

Teamgeist

Die Wahl des richtigen Partners ist nicht immer einfach, vor allem bei Expeditionen, die mehrere Monate dauern.

Es mag paradox erscheinen, aber das Basislager wird sehr schnell eng, obwohl man sich in der unendlich weiten Natur aufhält. Die Spannungen nehmen Tag für Tag zu, das Zusammenleben wird immer schwieriger. Je grösser das Team ist, desto mehr akzentuiert sich das Problem. Vor allem aus diesem Grund breche ich heute nur noch im ganz kleinen Team auf.

Das Team Troillet-Loretan verkörpert im Himalaya-Bergsteigen zweifellos die Seilschaft, die am längsten gehalten hat. Dass dies möglich war, ist nicht einem Wunderrezept, sondern nur ein paar einfachen Regeln zu verdanken.

Die manchmal beängstigende Stille im Basislager wird kaum durch lange Gespräche gestört. Jean und ich sind sehr verschieden. Wir versuchen gar nicht, uns besser kennenzulernen, unsere gemeinsamen Erfahrungen reichen. Als Alpinisten, die oft eher introvertiert sind, sprechen wir manchmal tagelang nicht miteinander. Es gelingt uns, eine gewisse Spannung aufzubauen, denn in der Handlung sind wir wie zwei perfekt aufeinander abgestimmte Maschinen. Am Tag «X» tauschen wir noch weniger Worte aus, denn theoretische Gespräche beflügeln nie…

Jean und ich teilen die gleiche Einstellung zum Bergsteigen, wir haben die gleiche Motivation und sind von den gleichen Strategien überzeugt. Das ist das einfache Rezept, das unseren langen gemeinsamen Weg ermöglichte.

Teamspirit

The choice of a climbing partner, especially for expeditions of a few months, is never easy.

It may seem paradoxical that although surrounded by a vast wilderness, the area of a base camp can seem terribly restricted. The greater the numbers, the greater the tensions that arise, and living daily in close proximity can become increasingly difficult. For this reason, nowadays I set out on my trips with a very small party.

The Troillet-Loretan team has undoubtedly been the longest-lasting partnership in the Himalaya. It has not grown out of any miracle, but simply out of a mutual respect for a few simple rules.

The occasionally distressing silence around our base camp is very rarely disturbed by lengthy discussions. Jean's character and mine are essentially very different. It is our way of life that counts, and we do not need to seek any deeper examination of each other. As climbers we are both generally withdrawn and reflective, and it often happens that a day or two may pass without any conversation between us. We manage to sustain a similar level of suspense, and, when the time comes, we are like two machines functioning at precisely the same pitch. Speculation being of less value than actio there is rarely any exchange of words between us on D-day.

Jean and I share the same concept of mountains, our motivation, and our conviction of the methods to be adopted are identical. That is the secret of our long spell together.

Ascension du pilier ouest du Makalu (8463 m). Troillet-Loretan, octobre 1991.

Im Oktober 1991 begeht Erhard Loretan mit Jean Troillet den Westpfeiler am Makalu (8463 m).

Ascent of the West pillar of Makalu (8463 m) Troillet-Loretan, October 1991.

Face sud du Shisha Pangma (8046 m). Tibet
Südwand des Shisha Pangma (8046 m). Tibet.
South face of Shisha Pangma (8046 m). Tibet

De nos jours, l'un des grands défis reste la traversée du Lhotse (8516 m) en technique légère.
Die Überschreitung des Lhotse (8516 m) im Alpinstil ist eines der ungelösten Probleme des Himalaya-Bergsteigens.
One of the greatest Himalayan challenges at present is an Alpine style traverse of the various summits of Lhotse (8516 m).

L'alpinisme et la compétition

Fort heureusement, l'alpinisme n'entre pas dans la catégorie des sports de compétition. Ce qui nous permet d'échapper à certaines règles matérialistes qui régissent le sport actuel.

Dans notre discipline, nous cherchons à innover, nous convoitons de nouvelles voies et gardons nos projets secrets le plus longtemps possible, pour une simple question de fierté. Mais si nous nous faisons doubler, tant pis, c'est de bonne guerre.

En alpinisme, on ne peut pas véritablement établir un classement hiérarchique. En effet, on ne peut jamais juger deux ascensions sur des terrains mixtes car, d'un jour à l'autre, voire d'une heure à l'autre, les conditions peuvent sensiblement changer.

Néanmoins, on déplore quelques malhonnêtes qui, pour diverses raisons, omettent sciemment certains détails, sans importance pour le grand public mais capitaux aux yeux des connaisseurs. Ainsi, dans un journal dit «spécialisé» nos voisins français se sont risqués à établir le «top 50» de «l'espèce grimpante»! Et ils n'y sont pas allés avec le dos de la cuiller. A tel point qu'ils ont logé à la même enseigne des athlètes qui se consacrent uniquement à l'escalade sportive et des adeptes de hauts sommets. C'est un non-sens que je tenais à relever.

Alpinismus und Wettkampf

Zum grossen Glück zählt der Alpinismus nicht zu den Wettkampfsportarten. Dadurch entgehen wir einigen materialistischen Regeln, die den Sport heute beherrschen.

Wir versuchen, innovativ zu sein, es gelüstet uns nach neuen Routen, und unsere Projekte halten wir – aus Gründen des Stolzes – so lange wie möglich geheim. Ist jemand anderer schneller als wir – nun, das ist durchaus recht so.

Im Alpinismus kann man kein echtes, gültiges Klassement aufstellen. So können beispielsweise zwei Besteigungen im kombinierten Gelände nicht miteinander verglichen werden, da sich die Verhältnisse von einem Tag zum anderen – oder gar von einer Stunde zur anderen – empfindlich verändern können.

Bedauerlicherweise gibt es aber doch ein paar Unehrliche, die aus verschiedenen Gründen bewusst Einzelheiten verschweigen, die für die grosse Öffentlichkeit unwichtig, für den Kenner aber von kapitaler Bedeutung sind. So wurde in einer Fachzeitschrift aus dem benachbarten Ausland eine Rangliste der fünfzig besten Bergsteiger präsentiert! Und dabei ging man nicht gerade zimperlich vor: So waren Athleten, die sich nur dem Sportklettern widmen, in der gleichen Kategorie wie Höhenbergsteiger klassiert… Ein Unsinn, den ich einmal beim Namen nennen wollte.

The competitive instinct

Fortunately, climbing does not belong to the category of competitive sports. This allows climbers to steer clear of the competitive attitudes which rule over almost all other sports today. In our branch of sport we seek novelty, we aspire after new routes, and, for reasons of personal gratification, we keep our activities quiet as long as possible. If some choose to act deceitfully, suggesting a state of war, that's just too bad.

Climbing is not an activity in which it would be meaningful to establish a ranking-list of performers. For the simple reason that on different days, or even at different hours on the same day, conditions could alter substantially during two separate ascents over much the same mixed ground.

I deplore the practice of some unscrupulous individuals who, for various reasons of their own, avoid mentioning details of their climbs, which are not of much importance to the general public, but of vital importance to the expert. A certain exclusive climbing magazine has ventured to set up a list of the climbing fraternity's «Top 50». And, as if that were not enough, they have judged by the same standards the performances of athletes, which are confined exclusively to technical climbs on walls, with the mountaineering achievements of experts on major mountain peaks. I regard this as pure nonsense.

L'un des meilleurs moments de la vie du camp de base: admirer les derniers rayons du soleil.
Die letzten Sonnenstrahlen: einer der schönsten Momente im Basislager.
One of the most beautiful moments of Base camp life: to watch the last rays of sunset.

Escalade au Nameless Tower, 6257 m
Kletterei am Nameless Tower (6257 m)
Ascent of the Nameless Tower, 6257 m (Trango Group)

Aventure extraordinaire sur ce mur vertical de 1200 m. Quatorze jours d'escalade sur un granit fabuleux pour ouvrir un nouvel itinéraire dans les Tours du Trango avec Voytek Kurtyka, alpiniste polonais.

An dieser senkrechten 1200-Meter-Mauer erlebte ich ein grossartiges Abenteuer: vierzehn Klettertage in wunderbarem Granit, in denen ich mit dem polnischen Alpinisten Voytek Kurtyka eine neue Route eröffnete.

An extraordinary adventure with the Polish climber Voytek Kurtyka. It took us 14 days to open a new route on this 1200 m vertical wall of superb granite.

Le camp de base
Das Basislager
Base camp

La vie au camp de base est très vite rébarbative. L'attente du départ engendre des tensions qu'il faut contrôler en s'occupant avec les moyens du bord.

Das Leben im Basislager wird sehr schnell unangenehm; das Warten auf den Aufbruch erzeugt Spannungen, die man mit den vorhandenen Mitteln bewältigen muss.

Life soon tends to become prett confined. The need to wait for the right moment for departure creates tensions, which need to be overcome with only limited means available.

Les populations locales

La notion de découverte revêt pour moi une très grande importance. Approche d'autres gens, d'autres cultures, d'autres façons de vivre et de penser. Avec la plupart des populations locales, je communique en anglais, langue que presque tous les enfants ont désormais la possibilité d'apprendre à l'école.

Dans les villages du Népal et du Pakistan, la vie est très rudimentaire. Les habitants travaillent uniquement pour assurer l'essentiel: le manger et le minimum vital. Ils possèdent un lopin de terre qu'ils cultivent afin d'assurer la récolte de riz pour l'année. Le travail dans les champs n'est pas mécanisé, les bœufs tirent encore la charrue. Ils sont à des années-lumière de notre civilisation décadente. Ils ne se rendent sans doute pas compte qu'ils possèdent un trésor remarquable: le temps. Ces indigènes connaissent encore les vraies valeurs de la vie et n'ont pas besoin d'artifices pour se mettre en valeur. Ils sont beaux et purs, tout simplement.

De leur côté, les Tibétains vivent sur les hauts plateaux désertiques. Il est difficile de leur donner un âge, car le climat vieillit leur peau prématurément. Bien que les frontières soient de nouveau ouvertes depuis quelques années, la pression chinoise accentue la précarité de leur situation. Pour certains, l'exil est la seule possibilité de survie.

Malheureusement, les Tibétains ne parlent pas d'autres langues que la leur, si bien que le contact avec eux ne peut être que visuel ou gestuel. Ils dégagent néanmoins une telle aura que les mots deviennent superflus.

Die einheimische Bevölkerung

Der Begriff des «Entdeckens» hat für mich einen sehr hohen Stellenwert. Dabei geht es um das Entdecken von anderen Menschen, anderen Kulturen, anderen Lebens- und Denkarten. Mit den meisten Einheimischen verständige ich mich auf Englisch, der Sprache, die die meisten Kinder heute in der Schule lernen können.

In den Dörfern Nepals und Pakistans ist das Leben sehr einfach. Die Bewohner arbeiten für die Nahrung und das Lebensnotwendige. Sie besitzen ein kleines Stück Land, das sie bebauen, um für das ganze Jahr genug Reis und Getreide zu haben. Die Feldarbeit ist nicht mechanisiert, die Pflüge werden noch von Rindern gezogen. Diese Menschen sind Lichtjahre von unserer Zivilisation entfernt. Sie sind sich sicher nicht bewusst, dass sie über ein bemerkenswertes Gut verfügen: die Zeit. Sie kennen noch die wahren Werte des Lebens und brauchen keine Tricks, um sich zur Geltung zu bringen; in ihrer Einfachheit sind sie schön und rein.

Die Tibeter ihrerseits leben auf wüstenähnlichen Hochebenen. Man kann ihr Alter schlecht schätzen, denn das harte Klima lässt die Haut vorzeitig altern. Zwar sind die Grenzen zu Tibet seit ein paar Jahren wieder offen, doch der chinesische Druck verschärft die heikle Lage. Vielen Tibetern bleibt als einzige Überlebenschance nur noch der Weg ins Exil.

Leider sprechen die Tibeter meist keine andere als ihre Muttersprache, so dass es beim Blickkontakt oder beim Austausch von Gesten bleibt. Ihre Ausstrahlung macht Worte allerdings überflüssig ...

The local people

The idea of ascertaining something new has always been of great interest to me. Such as encountering different cultures and their way of life and thought. Communication with most local populations is in English, the language which almost all children in future will have the opportunity to learn at school.

The life of an average villager in Nepal or Pakistan is very simple. The inhabitants work in their fields to provide themselves with their basic needs. With small land-holdings they strive to cultivate cereal crops in order to sustain their yearly requirements of foodgrains. There is no mechanisation and bullocks are used to till the soil. Their simple ways are an enlightening reflection on our decadent civilisation. It is doubtful if they are aware of the precious gift which they possess – ample time. These village dwellers, concerned with the real values in their daily lives, have no need for trivialities. They are pure and kindly folk.

On the other side of the border the Tibetans dwell on their lofty plateaux. Their ages are difficult to tell because of the harsh climate which wrinkles their skin prematurely. Although the frontiers were re-opened a few years ago, their situation remains precarious. For some Tibetans the only means of survival is by going into exile.

Tibetans, unfortunately, cannot speak any language other than their own, so that it is possible to communicate with them only by signs and gestures. But they possess an aura which makes speech almost superfluous.

Un coucher de soleil magique. Pourtant notre angoisse augmente, dans quelques instants la nuit rendra le froid encore plus vif et l'orientation difficile. Kangchenjunga 1995.

Magischer Sonnenuntergang am Kangchenjunga (1995); unsere Angst nimmt aber zu, denn die einbrechende Nacht verschärft die Kälte und erschwert die Orientierung.

A magical sunset. But our anxiety mounts; in a short time it will become intensely cold, and darkness will make route-finding difficult. Kangchenjunga 1995.

Neige profonde
　Tiefschnee
Deep snow

Tracer dans la neige profonde est sans doute l'obstacle le plus difficile à surmonter.
Das Spuren im Tiefschnee ist sicherlich das grösste Hindernis auf dem Weg zum Gipfel.
Forcing a path through deep snow poses one of the hardest problems.

Choix de l'itinéraire
Wahl der Route
Choice of route

Pour moi, simplement atteindre
le sommet n'est pas le plus important.
Le gravir par une belle ligne est
beaucoup plus attrayant.

Das Erreichen des Gipfels ist
für mich nicht das Wichtigste –
viel verlockender ist es, ihn über
eine schöne Linie zu besteigen.

I am always more attracted
by the choice of a fine route
than in merely reaching the summit.

Les transports

Les chemins d'accès au pied des géants himalayens sont généralement très longs. Nous séjournons environ un mois dans les divers camps de base. Et même si aujourd'hui je ne pars plus qu'en petite équipe, c'est près de huit cents kilos de nourriture et de matériel qu'il s'agit de transporter.

Au départ des capitales, les réseaux routiers se sont beaucoup développés ces dernières années. Pour ma part, je considère cette partie initiale comme la phase la plus dangereuse de l'expédition. Les chutes de pierres sont fréquentes, sans parler de l'état des véhicules. J'ai bien le goût du risque, mais pour autant que je puisse garder le contrôle de la situation… Ce n'est pas tout à fait l'impression que vous laisse ce chauffeur de bus, au volant depuis plus de vingt heures et qui lutte contre le sommeil en fumant du haschisch…

Au terminus des pistes, seules nos jambes nous permettront d'avancer. Pour acheminer notre matériel jusqu'aux camps de base, il y a plusieurs moyens, qui diffèrent selon les régions et le terrain. L'âne est très utilisé au Pakistan. Au Népal et au Tibet, le yack règne en maître. Il s'agit d'un animal incroyablement agile et résistant, qui monte jusqu'à 6000 m d'altitude et qui est capable de porter des charges d'une centaine de kilos, sans sourciller.

Les porteurs népalais ne sont pas moins impressionnants. Ils portent les charges au moyen d'une simple lanière passée autour de la tête. Pour un touriste bien entraîné, porter une charge de trente kilos représente déjà une belle performance. J'ai vu des gars transporter des charges de 120 kilos, pendant plusieurs jours…

Die Transportmittel

Der Anmarsch zu den Himalaya-Giganten ist normalerweise sehr lang, und im Basislager verbringen wir jeweils fast einen Monat. Auch wenn ich heute nur noch im Kleinteam aufbreche, müssen gegen 800 Kilo Lebensmittel und Material ins Basislager transportiert werden.

Das Strassennetz rund um die Hauptstädte wurde in den letzten Jahren stark verbessert. Ich empfinde die Anfangsphase einer Expedition als die gefährlichste: Steinschlag und Erdrutsche sind häufig, vom Zustand der Fahrzeuge wollen wir gar nicht erst reden. Ich schätze zwar das Risiko, möchte aber zugleich die Kontrolle über die Situation nicht verlieren – diesen Eindruck hat man nicht gerade bei einem Busfahrer, der seit über zwanzig Stunden am Steuer sitzt und Haschisch rauchend gegen den Schlaf kämpft!

Vom Ende der Strassen oder Naturpisten an sind unsere Beine das einzige Mittel, um weiterzukommen. Je nach Gegend und Gelände gibt es verschiedene Transportmittel, um unser Material in das Basislager zu schaffen: In Pakistan werden oft Esel als Trageteire benützt, in Nepal und Tibet ist es vor allem das Yak, ein unglaublich gewandtes und robustes Tier, das bis auf 6000 m aufsteigt und – ohne sich etwas anmerken zu lassen – Lasten bis über 100 Kilo trägt.

Nicht weniger eindrücklich sind die nepalesischen Träger: Sie tragen die Lasten mit Hilfe einer Art Stirnband, das sie um den Kopf legen. Wenn ein gut trainierter Tourist eine Last von 30 Kilo trägt, ist das schon eine hervorragende Leistung; ich habe aber Einheimische gesehen, die während mehrerer Tage Lasten von 120 Kilo schleppen …

Transport

Travelling to the foot of the Himalayan giants involves a long approach march. About a month is generally spent camping out and at base camp. Nowadays, although I travel with only small groups, there are still about 800 kilos of food and equipment which need to be transported.

Beyond the main cities, the towns and villages encountered on the way have developed considerably in recent years. This preliminary stage of the journey into the mountains strikes me as being the most dangerous phase of an expedition. The vehicles used are usually in deplorable condition and landslides are frequent. Added to these hazards is the unpredictability of hashish-smoking drivers struggling to avoid dropping off to sleep after 20 hours at the wheel. Despite my taste for risk-taking, I am always uncomfortable unless I know that I have the situation under my own control.

On reaching the end of the road further progress is made on foot and by using animal transport to get ourselves and our equipment to base camp. There are several options available, depending upon the region and the type of country. Porters and donkeys or mules are commonly used in Pakistan. In Nepal and Tibet the yak reigns supreme, an incredible animal, tough and agile, perfectly at home at altitudes above 6000 m, and capable of carrying a load of 100 kilos effortlessly.

No less impressive are the Nepalese porters who carry loads of about 30 kilos by means of a simple leather or bamboo strap attached to the forehead – a performance that would be considered remarkable even for an athletic tourist. I have seen some lads carrying loads of up to 120 kilos for several days …

La face ouest du Gasherbrum IV (7925 m, Karakoram) est l'une des grandes réalisations de ces quinze dernières années. Kurtyka-Schauer, été 1985.

Die Begehung der Westwand am Gasherbrum IV (7925 m, Karakorum) war eine der herausragendsten Leistungen der letzten 15 Jahre (Voytek Kurtyka und Robert Schauer, Sommer 1985).

The West face of Gasherbrum IV (7925 m) one of the great climbing achievements of recent years by Kurtyka - Schauer, Summer 1985.

Pollué, l'Himalaya?

Les polémiques au sujet des immondices rassemblées au pied des géants himalayens ne manquent pas. Elles font couler passablement d'encre. Il est évidemment aisé d'aller photographier une boîte de conserve au pied de l'Everest. Il en va autrement d'un sous-marin atomique coulé au fond de l'Antarctique…

Par la fascination qu'il suscite, l'Everest draine un nombre impressionnant de touristes. On en dénombre plus de trente mille par année dans la vallée du Khumbu menant à son pied. C'est vrai, le respect de l'environnement ne représente malheureusement pas toujours leur première préoccupation. Mais parmi eux, il faut savoir qu'une centaine de personnes seulement tenteront l'ascension du sommet.

La sonnette d'alarme a été tirée et une vive réaction s'en est suivie. Les gouvernements ont pris des mesures draconiennes. Ainsi une caution de 3000 $ est exigée au départ d'une expédition. On ne la récupère que si tous les détritus sont ramenés en plaine.

La vallée du Khumbu est bientôt plus propre que la Suisse, c'est tout dire! A mon avis, nous sommes passés d'un extrême à l'autre. Dire qu'il n'est même plus autorisé de brûler un bout de papier! Une mesure que j'ai quelque peine à comprendre en regard de la passivité irresponsable manifestée trop souvent par rapport aux véritables catastrophes écologiques. Je suis pourtant bien conscient de l'utilité de mesures de protection. Des gestes modestes, faciles à mettre en œuvre, ne coûtent pas cher. Et ils peuvent servir d'exemples.

Ist der Himalaya verschmutzt?

Die Polemiken im Zusammenhang mit der Verschmutzung am Fuss der Himalaya-Riesen reissen nicht ab und lassen viel Tinte fliessen. Natürlich ist es einfach, eine Konservenbüchse am Fuss des Everest zu fotografieren. Das ist im Fall eines unter der Antarktis aufgelaufenen Atom-U-Bootes etwas schwieriger…

Der Everest zieht wegen der Faszination, die er ausübt, eine beeindruckende Zahl von Touristen an. Im Khumbu, dem Tal an seinem Fuss, zählt man jährlich über 30 000 Besucher. Tatsächlich stellt die Achtung vor der Umwelt leider nicht immer ihre Hauptsorge dar. Unter ihnen versuchen aber nur etwa hundert Personen die Besteigung des Gipfels.

Die Alarmglocke wurde geläutet und löste eine starke Reaktion aus. Die Regierungen haben drakonische Massnahmen ergriffen. So wird in Nepal am Anfang einer Expedition eine Kaution von 3000 Dollar verlangt. Man erhält sie nur zurück, wenn alle Abfälle zurückgeführt werden.

Das Khumbu ist bald sauberer als die Schweiz – das sagt alles! Meiner Meinung nach sind wir von einem Extrem zum anderen übergegangen: So darf nicht einmal mehr ein Stück Papier verbrannt werden! Eine Massnahme, mit der ich Mühe habe, wenn ich an die unverantwortliche Passivität denke, die oft bei echten ökologischen Katastrophen zu beobachten ist. Natürlich bin ich mir der Nützlichkeit von Schutzmassnahmen durchaus bewusst: Bescheidene Handlungen, die einfach durchgeführt werden können, kosten nicht viel und wirken beispielhaft.

Pollution in the Himalaya?

A lot of ink has flowed, and endless argument has taken place, over the growing accumulation of rubbish at the foot of major Himalayan mountains. Obviously, it is perfectly easy for the media to photograph an empty tin at the foot of Everest; it would be quite another matter had the object been an atomic submarine sunk in the depths of the Antarctic.

Owing to its special attraction, Everest draws huge crowds of tourists, about 30'000 of whom pass through the Khumbu valley at the foot of the mountain each year. Unfortunately, respect for the environment is not one of their prime concerns. Amongst their numbers, there are perhaps only about 100 people who go there actually to try to climb to the top.

The alarm signals having been sounded, a sharp reaction has followed, and draconian measures have been introduced by the Government of Nepal. Under these, each expedition upon departure must deposit between 3000 U.S. dollars, which is refundable only if it can establish, through lengthy administrative procedures, that all rubbish has been carried down.

The Khumbu valley will soon be cleaner than Switzerland, so they say. It seems as if the authorities want to go from one extreme to another, now even banning the burning of a scrap of paper! A measure which I find hard to understand given the irresponsible attitude too often shown towards major ecological disasters. Naturally, I agree that measures to protect the environment are essential, but more modest and less costly schemes, simple to operate, would probably serve the purpose more effectively.

Bivouac à 6900m lors de la tentative de 1997 sur la traversée du Nanga Parbat (8125 m) avec Voytek Kurtyka.

Biwak auf 6900 m am Nanga Parbat (8125 m) beim Versuch der Überschreitung mit Voytek Kurtyka, Sommer 1997.

Bivouac at 6900 m during an attempt to traverse the Mazeno ridge of Nanga Parbat (8125 m) with Voytek Kurtyka in 1997.

Avalanches
Lawinen
Avalanches

Une des choses qui m'impressionnent le plus sur ces montagnes himalayennes est la dimension des avalanches.
Die Dimensionen der Lawinen im Himalaya beeindrucken mich ganz besonders.
One of the most impressive features of the Himalaya is the gigantic scale of the avalanches.

La recherche scientifique

D'énormes moyens ont été mis en œuvre par des scientifiques pour tenter d'élucider certains mystères de la vie en montagne. Des chercheurs ont même installé de véritables laboratoires à près de 8000 m d'altitude. Je reste pourtant convaincu qu'on ne saura jamais où se situent les limites humaines car tous les tests, aussi poussés soient-ils, manquent de réalisme. Je suis persuadé qu'on ne peut pas évaluer scientifiquement l'influence de l'état psychique des sujets analysés.

Il y a un monde entre la tension psychologique d'une cordée seule dans la face nord de l'Everest et celle de deux alpinistes escaladant la voie normale, entourée d'autres alpinistes et d'une équipe médicale. Les deux individus de la face nord savent pertinemment qu'en cas d'ennui ils pourraient avoir de la peine à sauver leur peau. Il en va tout autrement des deux «cobayes» de la voie normale!

Pour parvenir à des résultats fiables, il faudrait simuler et jauger de multiples facteurs: le froid, le vent, la tension psychologique, le sommeil, la sous-alimentation, la motivation, l'éloignement. Pour l'heure, une chose tombe sous le sens: la très haute altitude n'est pas viable à long terme. Un peu d'expérience et de bon sens valent mieux que d'importantes études. Le meilleur remède à l'œdème consiste toujours à rester raisonnable en toute occasion et à savoir redescendre à temps.

Die Forschung

Wissenschaftler haben riesige Mittel in Bewegung gesetzt, um ein paar Geheimnisse des Lebens in den Bergen zu erleuchten – dazu wurden auf fast 8000 m wahre Forschungslabors eingerichtet. Ich bin aber nach wie vor überzeugt, dass man nie wissen wird, wo die menschlichen Grenzen liegen: Allen noch so ausgeklügelten wissenschaftlichen Versuchen fehlt es nämlich letztlich an Wirklichkeitsnähe. Ich bin überzeugt, dass man den Einfluss des psychischen Zustandes auf die untersuchten Subjekte nicht wissenschaftlich messen kann.

Zwischen der psychologischen Anspannung einer Seilschaft, die sich allein in der Everest-Nordflanke befindet, und jener von zwei Alpinisten, die – umgeben von anderen Bergsteigern und einem medizinischen Team – über die Normalroute aufsteigen, liegen Welten. Die zwei Menschen in der Nordflanke sind sich ständig bewusst, dass sie eine schwierige Situation vielleicht nicht oder nur mit Mühe überleben. Bei den zwei «Kandidaten» auf der Normalroute liegt die Sache ganz anders!

Um zuverlässige Resultate zu erreichen, müsste man zahlreiche Faktoren simulieren und messen können: Kälte, Wind, psychologische Spannung, Schlaf, unzureichende Ernährung, Motivation, Abgeschiedenheit. Ganz klar auf der Hand liegt nur, dass der Mensch auf grosser Höhe nicht lange überleben kann. Etwas Erfahrung und der gesunde Menschenverstand zählen mehr als bedeutende Studien. Das beste Vorbeugemittel gegen ein Ödem ist immer noch, ständig vernünftig zu bleiben und rechtzeitig abzusteigen.

High altitude research

A vast amount of scientific work has been carried out to try to resolve various physical problems associated with high mountains. Some researchers have gone as far as setting up a virtual laboratory at almost 8000 m. Whilst some of the results have been interesting, the tests, however, extended they may be, lack realism in attempting to define human limits, because I am convinced that psychological factors cannot be determined by scientific tests alone.

There is a world of difference between the psychological tension involved in a solitary team climbing the North Face of Everest and in that of two climbers ascending the normal route, accompanied by a support party and a medical unit. The two alone on the North Face know perfectly well that if anything should go wrong, their lives would be in extreme danger – a situation totally different from that of the two «guinea-pigs» on the normal route.

In order to obtain viable results, the tests would have to include a variety of diverse factors – temperature, wind strength, psychological stress, lack of sleep, insufficient food and drink, personal motivation, isolation. At present, the one thing that we know for certain is that the high-altitude zone is not one in which to hang around. Experience and common sense are of greater value than extended studies. The best remedy for high-altitude oedema will always be to exercise good sense whatever the situation, kuowing exactly when the time has come to descend.

Ambiance chimérique. Pangboche, Khumbu, Népal.
Geheimnisvolle Stimmung in Pangboche, Khumbu, Nepal.
Grotesque atmosphere Pangboche, Khumbu, Nepal.

La montagne mystique

Il n'y a pas si longtemps, les sommets himalayens étaient réservés aux dieux. Le côté mystique de ces hauts lieux revêtait une telle importance qu'il ne laissait personne indifférent. L'homme blanc qui profanait ces endroits pouvait être rendu responsable de tout déséquilibre de la nature.

Dans les Alpes, n'avons-nous pas suivi le même cheminement? La montagne était à craindre jusqu'au jour où les alpinistes anglais, accompagnés par des guides indigènes, l'eurent démystifiée. A l'instar de ce qui s'est passé chez nous il y a quelques décennies, les ascensions himalayennes tendent à se banaliser.

Le sherpa est devenu le guide qui emmène son client sur les plus hauts sommets. C'est un spécialiste de la haute altitude qui fait un travail remarquable, malheureusement insuffisamment considéré. Le sherpa travaille dans l'ombre; son aide demeure un sujet tabou. Je le considère quant à moi comme un compagnon qui contribue à la réussite d'une entreprise.

Tous les sherpas ne sont pas guides. La majorité d'entre eux se contentent de collaborer avec les touristes. Ils sont hommes d'affaires, restaurateurs, cuisiniers ou plongeurs. L'himalayisme s'étant considérablement développé, les populations locales essaient d'en tirer le meilleur parti.

Geheimnisvolle Berge

Noch vor nicht allzu langer Zeit waren die Gipfel des Himalaya den Göttern vorbehalten – ihre mystische Ausstrahlung war so stark, dass sie niemanden unberührt liess. Der weisse Mensch, der diese Stätten dann entweihte, konnte für jegliches Ungleichgewicht in der Natur verantwortlich gemacht werden.

Haben wir in den Alpen nicht den gleichen Prozess miterlebt? Man fürchtete sich vor den Bergen bis zu jenem Tag, an dem die britischen Bergsteiger – begleitet von einheimischen Bergführern – sie entmystifizierten. Wie es bei uns vor ein paar Jahrzehnten in den Alpen geschah, so werden heute auch die Besteigungen von Himalaya-Gipfeln alltäglicher und banaler.

Der Sherpa ist zum Führer geworden, der seinen Gast auf die höchsten Gipfel begleitet. Er kennt sich auf extremer Höhe bestens aus und leistet bemerkenswerte Arbeit, die oft zu wenig beachtet wird. Die Sherpas arbeiten oft im Schatten, ihre Unterstützung wird verschwiegen. Was mich betrifft, so betrachte ich sie als Gefährten, die wesentlich zum Erfolg einer Unternehmung beitragen.

Natürlich sind nicht alle Sherpas Führer; die meisten unter ihnen begnügen sich mit der Zusammenarbeit mit den Touristen. Sie sind Geschäftsmänner, Wirte, Köche oder Tellerwäscher. Die Einheimischen versuchen ganz einfach, aus dem Himalaya-Tourismus, der beachtlich zugenommen hat, das Beste zu ziehen.

Mystical mountains

Not very long ago, Himalayan summits were believed to be the abode of gods. Such was the mystical aspect of those lofty places that there were few who regarded them with indifference. The white man, by treating them irreverently, was believed to be responsible for every disorder in the natural environment.

Have we not passed through a similar phase in the Alps? Mountains used to be regarded as objects of dread, until the day when climbers from England, accompanied by local guides, unveiled their mysteries. Like the developments that have taken place in the Alps over the past 70–80 years, climbing in the Himalaya has now become fairly commonplace.

Sherpas have adopted the rôle of guides, leading clients to the tops of the highest peaks. They are high-altitude specialists who excel in their work, which, I think, tends to be underestimated. Working in the background, the extent of their contribution often tends to be obscured. I have always regarded them as partners, contributing fully to the success of an enterprise.

Not all Sherpas take up the guiding profession. Most of them prefer to join parties of tourists. Some set themselves up in business, or open restaurants, or take up service in hotels. The local population, understandably, endeavour to take the best possible advantage of the huge expansion in Himalayan climbing and tourism.

Camp de base de la face nord de l'Everest. Ces formations de glace s'élevant jusqu'à 30 m sont des pénitents.

Basislager auf der Everest-Nordseite; die bis zu 30 Meter hohen Formationen werden Büsserschnee genannt.

Our base camp for the ascent of the North face of Everest. These glacial pinnacles attain heights of up to 30 m.

L'une de mes plus belles escalades: la tour sans nom au Trango.
Eine meiner schönsten Klettereien: der Nameless Tower (Trango Tower).
One of my finest climbs: the Nameless Tower (Trango Group).

Après deux mois d'expédition, petite relaxation dans les sources d'eau chaude sulfureuse de Chongo (Baltoro, Pakistan).
Nach zwei Expeditionsmonaten Entspannung im warmen Wasser der Schwefelquellen von Chongo (Baltoro, Pakistan).
Relaxing in the warm sulphurous spring at Chongo after a two-month expedition (Baltoro Glacier, Pakistan).

L'himalayisme, demain

L'Himalaya offre encore de multiples possibilités d'expéditions extraordinaires: des parois vierges, de grandes traversées, des enchaînements.

Aujourd'hui, les expéditions sportives qui apportent une réelle contribution à l'évolution de l'himalayisme sont rares. Les prix exorbitants exigés par certains gouvernements expliquent en partie cela. Mais il faut bien admettre que, depuis quelques années, on assiste à un manque flagrant de créativité.

Les limites physiologiques du corps humain posent problème. On ne sait pas encore s'il est possible de survivre 24 heures au sommet de l'Everest. Aujourd'hui, des projets peuvent se concrétiser, qui étaient encore impossibles hier. La traversée du Lhotse, que nous avions tentée en 1994, est à l'heure actuelle inimaginable en technique légère car il nous manque une donnée essentielle, celle de la durée de vie d'un être humain à plus de 8300 m d'altitude.

Il est difficile de prévoir ce que sera l'himalayisme demain. Je suis persuadé que les limites sont loin d'être atteintes. Je souhaite pour ma part que les prochaines générations optent systématiquement pour le style léger et sans oxygène. Et qu'importe si certains projets se révèlent irréalisables.

Die Zukunft des Höhenbergsteigens

Der Himalaya bietet noch zahlreiche Möglichkeiten für aussergewöhnliche Expeditionen: unberührte Wände, grosse Überschreitungen, Gipfelgruppen.

Heute gibt es nur wenige «sportliche» Expeditionen, die einen echten Beitrag zur Weiterentwicklung des Himalaya-Bergsteigens leisten. Die überrissenen Preise, die von gewissen Regierungen verlangt werden, erklären dies nur zum Teil: Seit ein paar Jahren kann man bei den Expeditionen einen offenkundigen Mangel an Kreativität beobachten.

Die physiologischen Grenzen des Menschen stellen Probleme: Man weiss noch nicht, ob man auf dem Gipfel des Everest 24 Stunden überleben kann. Wohl können heute Projekte verwirklicht werden, die gestern noch undenkbar waren. Die Überschreitung des Lhotse in leichtem Alpinstil, die wir 1994 versuchten, ist aber zur Zeit noch unvorstellbar, da uns eine wichtige Grösse nicht bekannt ist: Wie lange kann ein Mensch auf über 8300 m überleben?

Es ist schwierig, die Zukunft des Himalaya-Bergsteigens vorauszusehen. Ich bin überzeugt, dass die Grenzen noch bei weitem nicht erreicht sind, und wünsche mir, dass sich die nächsten Generationen für einen leichten Stil ohne Sauerstoffflaschen entscheiden. Und wen stört es, wenn sich gewisse Projekte als undurchführbar erweisen sollten!

The future outlook

There remains still a large variety of possibilities for extreme ventures in the Himalaya: unclimbed faces, traverses of major peaks, and linked ascents within major groups.

At the present time, technical ascents at very high levels, of the sort that would make a real contribution to the development of Himalayan climbing, seem to be rare. This could be explained partly because of the enormous peak-fees demanded by certain governments. But it has to be admitted that in recent years there appears to have been an obvious lack of imagination in the ambitions of Himalayan climbers.

There are still some unsolved problems concerning the physiological limits of the human body. It is not known for certain whether survival for 24 hours on the summit of Everest would be possible. Although today some projects are achievable which only a few years ago would have been considered impossible, a traverse of the main summits of Lhotse, which Jean and I attempted in 1994, is not conceivable in Alpine style, because we still lack some essential knowledge such as the duration of life expectancy at altitudes above 8300 m.

It is difficult to forecast what shape Himalayan climbing will take over the next few years. I am fairly sure that we are still some way from having reached man's absolute physical limits. Personally, I hope that coming generations will choose to adopt light-weight methods without the use of artificial oxygen, even though certain objectives might not be achievable by such means.

Tingri (4000 m, Tibet), dernier village avant le Cho Oyu (8201 m).

Tingri (4000 m, Tibet), das letzte Dorf vor dem Cho Oyu (8201 m).

Tingri 4000 m in Tibet, last village before Cho Oyu (8201 m).

Escalade glacière
Eiskletterei
Climbing glacier ice

Chez l'alpiniste, la vie ne tient pas qu'à un fil, mais aux lames de ses piolets et crampons ancrés de quelques centimètres.

Beim Alpinisten hängt das Leben nicht an einem Faden, sondern an den ein paar Zentimeter im Eis verankerten Zacken seiner Pickel und Steigeisen.

With the pick of his ice-axe and the spikes of his crampons penetrating a few centimeters of ice, the climber's life hangs upon a thread.

La flore
  Blumen
Flowers

Dans cette immensité de glace et de neige, un signe de vie, parfois même à plus de 5000 m.
Ein Zeichen des Lebens – manchmal auf über 5000 m – in den unendlichen Eis- und Schneewüsten.
A sign of living nature, sometimes at 5000 m, amidst a vast expanse of ice and snow.

L'Everest et l'argent

Tout au long du siècle, l'Everest n'a cessé de fasciner le monde. Ce sommet mythique engendre les ambitions et les projets les plus fous. D'aucuns engagent des sommes considérables et sont même prêts à payer de leur vie pour assouvir un fantasme. Par ailleurs, à voir à l'œuvre certaines expéditions inexpérimentées, dont les acteurs semblent ne jamais avoir vu de la neige de près, on s'interroge. Et on a parfois aussi l'impression que nombre de pays ne ménagent pas leurs efforts pour tenter de placer une cordée sur le toit du monde.

Aujourd'hui, à peu de choses près, une personne disposant de moyens financiers, d'une condition physique moyenne et d'une expérience quasiment nulle peut se «payer» l'Everest. Cet «alpiniste» va pouvoir engager six sherpas qui poussent, huit qui tirent et dix autres qui transportent la réserve d'oxygène, lui se contentant de se balader sans la moindre charge sur un itinéraire truffé de cordes fixes et d'échelles, de la base au sommet.

Si la nature l'a comblé et qu'il a atteint son objectif, il lui manque trop souvent l'honnêteté nécessaire pour mettre en évidence l'aide apportée par les sherpas et toute l'infrastructure mise en place. S'il réussit, il claironne bien haut son exploit. Dans le cas contraire, il pourra aller jusqu'à intenter un procès à son guide…

D'un côté, il y a le montagnard qui gravit l'Everest par ses propres moyens et sans oxygène; de l'autre, il y a l'assisté. Dans un cas seulement, on peut parler de performance…

Der Everest und das Geld

In diesem ganzen letzten Jahrhundert hat der Everest die Menschen fasziniert; dieser mystische Gipfel ruft Ambitionen und die verrücktesten Projekte ins Leben. Einige Bergsteiger investieren beträchtliche Summen und sind sogar bereit, mit ihrem Leben zu bezahlen, um eine Phantasievorstellung zu befriedigen. Man muss den Kopf schütteln beim Anblick gewisser unerfahrener Expeditionen, deren Akteure offenbar noch nie aus der Nähe Schnee gesehen haben. Manchmal hat man auch den Eindruck, dass einige Länder keine Mühe scheuen, eine Seilschaft auf das Dach der Welt zu bringen.

Heute sind wir fast so weit, dass sich eine Person, die über finanzielle Mittel, eine durchschnittliche physische Verfassung und so gut wie keine Erfahrung verfügt, den Everest «leisten» kann. Dieser «Bergsteiger» kann sechs Sherpas anstellen, die stossen, acht, die ziehen, und zehn weitere, die den Vorrat an Sauerstoffflaschen hochtragen – er selbst kann ohne die kleinste Last auf der vom Basislager bis zum Gipfel mit Fixseilen und Leitern gespickten Aufstiegsroute hochspazieren.

Wenn es die Natur gut mit ihm meint und er sein Ziel erreicht, fehlt es ihm oft an der nötigen Ehrlichkeit, um die Unterstützung durch die Sherpas und die vorhandene Infrastruktur hervorzuheben. Statt dessen posaunt er seinen Erfolg aus. Andernfalls, wenn er den Gipfel nicht erreicht, geht er unter Umständen so weit, seinem Bergführer einen Prozess anzuhängen …

Auf der einen Seite gibt es den wahren Bergsteiger, der den Everest mit eigenen Mitteln und ohne künstlichen Sauerstoff besteigt; auf der anderen Seite gibt es jenen, der sich unterstützen lässt. Von einer grossen Leistung kann man nur im einen Fall sprechen!

Money and Everest

Throughout this century, Everest has been a source of increasing fascination to the world. This fabled mountain has aroused all manner of wild ambitions and far-fetched projects. There are some who are prepared to hand over considerable sums of money, and even to pay with their lives, in order to gratify their daydream to reach the top. The presence of some expeditions is indeed surprising, composed of inexperienced persons some of whom may never before have approached the snowline. In addition, numerous countries appear to spare no efforts to ensure that a group of their climbers should stand on the roof of the world.

Today one might almost say that anyone with sufficient money at his disposal, possessing average physical ability, and with practically no experience, could pay his way to the top of Everest. This «climber» would be able to engage 6 sherpas to push him, 8 to pull him and 10 others to carry all his oxygen whilst he walked upwards, unburdened by any load, along a route festooned with fixed ropes and ladders from base to summit.

If the conditions are favourable and he achieves his goal, he will proudly proclaim his success and will probably not be honest enough to acknowledge to what extent it was due to the assistance provided by his Sherpas. In case of failure he could always bring an action against his guide.

Take a climber who ascends Everest by traditional methods without the aid of oxygen, and another who does so using oxygen and other assistance – the quality of the ascent has been good in only one case.

Dans la région de Nanga Parbat (Pakistan), c'est surtout l'âne qui transporte les charges.

In der Region des Nanga Parbat (Pakistan); hier werden vor allem Esel als Lasttiere eingesetzt.

In the Nanga Parbat region (Pakistan), donkeys are mostly used for transport of loads.

Le bivouac
Im Biwak
Bivouac

Combien de fois me suis-je dit que je serais mieux dans mon lit! Et pourtant les nuits passées dans les conditions les plus extrêmes constituent mes meilleurs souvenirs.

Wie oft habe ich mich nach meinem Bett gesehnt! Und doch gehören die Nächte, die ich unter extremsten Bedingungen verbracht habe, zu meinen besten Erinnerungen.

How many times have I told myself how much better off I would be in my own bed! And yet, I count the nights that I have spent under the most extreme conditions amongst my best memories.

La mort de près

Au cours de mes nombreuses expéditions, il m'est arrivé de côtoyer la mort. J'ai malheureusement perdu plusieurs collègues et amis en montagne. J'ai assisté à des drames terribles, vu la mort de près et senti son horrible odeur. Cependant, jamais je n'ai remis en question ma passion. A aucun instant je ne me suis laissé abattre.

Ce n'est pas que je sois insensible à la mort. J'ai vécu des périodes très douloureuses après la disparition d'un ami. Et pourtant, aussi surprenant que cela puisse paraître, j'estime que le drame fait partie des règles du jeu. Chacun sait qu'en haute altitude, une fois blessé, ses chances de survie sont quasi nulles.

Bien que je n'aie aucune envie de quitter ce monde, la manière de mourir m'inquiète plus que la mort elle-même.

Chaque expérience tragique nous rappelle à quel point l'être humain est vulnérable. Même les situations les plus dramatiques apportent leur lot d'enseignements. On peut toujours en retirer des éléments positifs, lesquels nous permettent de continuer. Jusqu'au jour où, fatalement, on commettra aussi l'erreur…

Die Nähe des Todes

Bei meinen zahlreichen Expeditionen habe ich den Tod mehrmals gestreift. Leider habe ich einige Kollegen und Freunde in den Bergen verloren; ich habe schreckliche Dramen erlitten, den Tod von nahe erlebt und seinen grässlichen Geschmack erfahren. Meine Leidenschaft habe ich aber deswegen nie in Frage gestellt. Ich habe keinen Augenblick daran gedacht, sie aufzugeben.

Natürlich bin ich dem Tod gegenüber nicht unempfindlich. Ich habe nach dem Verlust eines Freundes sehr schmerzliche Zeiten erlebt. Und dennoch – so überraschend es scheinen mag – glaube ich, dass das Drama zu den Spielregeln gehört. Jeder weiss, dass bei einer Verletzung, einem Unfall in grosser Höhe die Überlebenschancen fast gleich null sind.

Auch wenn ich überhaupt keine Lust habe, die Welt zu verlassen, beunruhigt mich die Art des Sterbens mehr als der Tod selbst.

Jede tragische Erfahrung erinnert uns daran, wie verletzlich der Mensch ist. Auch die dramatischsten Situationen bringen uns etwas bei. Man kann daraus immer positive Lehren ziehen, die uns das Weitergehen ermöglichen. Bis zu jenem Tag, an dem auch wir zwangsläufig einen entscheidenden Fehler begehen …

Nearness to death

During the course of my numerous expeditions I have sometimes found myself skirting the boundaries of death. Unfortunately, I have lost several friends and companions in the mountains, and I have witnessed some terrible tragedies, looking death in the face and experiencing its terrible stench. Yet I have never questioned the validity of my passion nor, for a moment, have I ever considered giving it up.

This is not because I am unaffected by the fear of death. The death of friends has caused me to suffer periods of deep grief. And yet, surprising though it may seem, I believe that tragedy is one of the rules of the game. Every mountaineer knows that any form of injury at high altitude is almost certain to prove fatal.

I have no wish to lose my life, but the manner of my death troubles me more than the prospect of death itself.

Every human tragedy makes us aware of the extent to which we are vulnerable as human beings. Lessons are to be learnt from even the most dramatic disaster. Through it we might be able to perceive some positive element, which adds to the resolve that enables us to continue. Until the day when, as others have done, we happen to commit a fatal error …

Camp de base du Makalu (8463 m, Népal).
Im Basislager des Makalu (8463 m, Nepal).
Base camp below Makalu (8463 m, Nepal).

Ambiances...
    Atmosphäre...
  Ambience...

On peut escalader maintes fois
la même montagne, mais ses caractéristiques
se modifient constamment.

Man kann den gleichen Berg immer
wieder besteigen, doch die Atmosphäre
ist jedesmal anders.

The same mountain may be climbed
several times, but the atmosphere
will always be different.

Camp à 6650 m lors de la traversée intégrale de l'Annapurna (8091 m). Octobre 1984. Joss-Loretan.
Zwischenlager auf 6650 m bei der Überschreitung der Annapurna (8091 m) mit Norbert Joss im Oktober 1984.
Camp at 6650 m on the East ridge during the first complete traverse of Annapurna (8091 m).

Notice biographique

Nom: **Erhard Loretan**

Date de naissance: **28.04.1959**

Adresse: **1653 Crésuz, Suisse**

Profession: **ébéniste (1979), guide de montagne (1981)**

Langue maternelle: **français**

Parle: **allemand, italien, anglais, espagnol**

Palmarès

1980: plusieurs premières dans les Andes.

1982: premier 8000 m, le Nanga Parbat (8125 m).

1983: trilogie en 17 jours au Baltoro: Gasherbrum II (8035 m), Gasherbrum I (8068 m) et Broad Peak (8047 m).

1984: Manaslu (8163 m) au printemps et première de l'arête Est de l'Annapurna (8091 m) en automne.

1985: deux tentatives dans la face Sud du K2 (8611 m), puis ascension de l'arête des Abruzzes en juillet. En décembre, première hivernale de la face Est du Dhaulagiri (8167 m).

1986: traversée de la «couronne impériale» dans les Alpes valaisannes: 38 sommets dont 30 à plus de 4000 m, en 19 jours et en hiver. En août, face Nord de l'Everest. En octobre, tentative dramatique dans la face Sud-Ouest du Cho Oyu (mort de Pierre-Alain Steiner).

1987: année sabbatique due à deux accidents graves.

1988: première en face Est du Nameless Tower au Trango (6257 m), Pakistan.

1989: en janvier, 13 faces Nord en 13 jours dans l'Oberland bernois, Suisse. Tentatives avortées dans la face Ouest du K2.

1990: première dans la face Sud-Ouest du Cho Oyu (8201 m) et, quelques jours plus tard, une autre première dans la face Sud du Shisha Pangma (8046 m), Tibet.

1991: tentative dans la face Ouest du Makalu et ascension du pilier Ouest (8463 m).

1992: tentatives avortées dans la face Ouest du K2.

1993: échec au Kangchenjunga (8586 m), Népal.

1994: ascension du Lhotse (8516 m), abandon du projet de la traversée sur le Lhotse Shar (8386 m). En décembre, première ascension du mont Epperly (4606 m) en solitaire, Antarctique.

1995: en octobre, ascension réussie du Kangchenjunga (8586 m). Loretan devient le troisième homme à avoir gravi les quatorze 8000 de la planète. En décembre, première ascension d'un sommet sans nom (4600 m) en Antarctique.

1996: plusieurs ascensions en solitaire sur des 6000 m au Tibet.

1997: tentative de la traversée du Mazeno-Ridge au Nanga Parbat.

1998: après plus de 25 expéditions, il était temps de consacrer une année aux Alpes et à mon métier de guide. En mai, Cotopaxi (5897 m) et Chimborazo (6310 m) en Equateur. Novembre-décembre, expédition prévue en Patagonie.

Biographische Angaben

Name:	**Erhard Loretan**
Geburtsdatum:	**28.04.1959**
Adresse:	**1653 Crésuz, Schweiz**
Beruf:	**Möbelschreiner (1979), Bergführer (1981)**
Muttersprache:	**Französisch**
Spricht:	**Deutsch, Italienisch, Englisch, Spanisch**

Alpinistisches Palmarès

1980: Mehrere Erstbegehungen in den Anden.

1982: Erster Achttausender-Gipfel: Nanga Parbat (8125 m).

1983: Baltoro-Trilogie innerhalb von 17 Tagen: Gasherbrum II (8035 m), Hidden Peak oder Gasherbrum I (8068 m) und Broad Peak (8047 m).

1984: Im Frühling Besteigung des Manaslu (8163 m) und im Herbst Erstbegehung des Ostgrates an der Annapurna (8091 m).

1985: Zwei Versuche an der K2-Südwand und im Juli Besteigung des K2 (8611 m) über den Abruzzi-Grat. Im Dezember erste Winterbegehung der Dhaulagiri-Ostwand (8167 m).

1986: Gruppe von 38 Gipfeln in den Walliser Alpen – darunter 30 Viertausender – im Winter und innerhalb von 19 Tagen. Im August Besteigung des Everest (8846 m) über die Nordflanke. Im Oktober dramatischer Versuch am Cho Oyu, bei dem Pierre-Alain Steiner ums Leben kommt.

1987: Wegen zwei schweren Unfällen pausiert E. Loretan.

1988: Neutour durch die Ostwand des Nameless Tower (6257 m) im Trango-Gebiet.

1989: Gruppe von 13 Nordwänden im Berner Oberland. Abgebrochener Versuch an der Westwand des K2.

1990: Erstbegehung der Südwestwand des Cho Oyu (8201 m) und wenige Tage später neue Route durch die Südwand des Shisha Pangma (8046 m).

1991: Versuch an der Makalu-Westwand und Begehung des Westpfeilers an diesem Gipfel (8463 m).

1992: Erfolgloser Versuch an der K2-Westwand.

1993: Misserfolg am Kangchenjunga (8586 m).

1994: Projekt der Überschreitung des Lhotse (8516 m) zum Lhotse Shar (8386 m) und Abbruch auf dem Gipfel des Lhotse. Erstbesteigung im Alleingang des Mount Epperly (4606 m) in der Antarktis.

1995: Im Oktober Erfolg am Kangchenjunga (8586 m). E. Loretan hat damit als dritter Mensch alle vierzehn Achttausender der Erde bestiegen. Im Dezember Erstbesteigung eines 4600 m hohen, namenlosen Gipfels in der Antarktis.

1996: Besteigung im Alleingang einiger Sechstausender in Tibet.

1997: Versuch der Überschreitung des Mazeno-Grates am Nanga Parbat.

1998: Nach mehr als 25 Expeditionen ist es Zeit, ein Jahr den Alpen und dem Bergführerberuf zu widmen. Im Mai Besteigung des Cotopaxi (5897 m) und des Chimborazo (6310 m) in Ecuador. Für November/Dezember ist eine Expedition in Patagonia.

Biographical details

Name: **Erhard Loretan**

Date of birth: **28.04.1959**

Address: **1653 Crésuz, Switzerland**

Profession: **carpenter (1979), mountain guide (1981)**

Mother tongue: **French**

Other languages: **German, Italian, English, Spanish**

List of main ascents

1980: Several first ascents in the Peruvian Andes

1982: First Swiss ascent of Nanga Parbat (8125 m).

1983: Ascended in 17 days three 8000 m peaks: Broad Peak (8047 m), Gasherbrum I (8068 m), Gasherbrum II (8035 m).

1984: Ascent of Manaslu (8163 m) during the spring, and the first complete ascent of the East ridge of Annapurna (8091 m) in the autumn.

1985: Two attempts on South face of K2 (8611 m) followed by ascent via S.E. (Abruzzi) ridge in July. First winter ascent of East face of Dhaulagiri (8167 m).

1986: Linked ascents of 38 alpine summits (30 above 4000 m) in 19 days during winter. In August, ascent of North face of Everest in 2 days. In October attempt on S.W. face of Cho Oyu (8201 m), and tragic death of Pierre-Alain Steiner.

1987: Sabbatical year, following two serious accidents.

1988: First ascent of East face of Nameless Tower (6257 m) Trango Group, Pakistan.

1989: In January, linked ascents of thirteen North faces in the Bernese Oberland. Attempt on West face of K2.

1990: First ascent of S.W. face of Cho Oyu (8201 m), followed a few days later by ascent of Shishapangma (8046 m) via new route on S. face.

1991: Attempt on W. face, and ascent of West pillar of Makalu (8463 m).

1992: Attempt on W. face of K2.

1993: Attempt on Kangchenjunga (8586 m).

1994: Ascent of Lhotse (8516 m), traverse to Lhotse Shar abandoned. First ascent of Mt. Epperly (4606 m, solo) in the Antarctic on 1 December.

1995: Ascent of Kangchenjunga 8586 m on 5 October, making Loretan the third climber to have ascended all of the world's fourteen mountains above 8000 m. In December, first ascent solo of Unnamed Peak (4600 m) in the Ellsworth Mountains, Antarctica.

1996: Several solo ascents of 6000 m peaks in Tibet.

1997: Attempt to traverse the 12-km-long Mazeno ridge of Nanga Parbat.

1998: After over 25 expeditions, a return to the European Alps in my professional capacity as a guide. Ascents in South America in May, Cotopaxi (5897 m), and Chimborazo (6310 m). Expeditions planned for winter of 1998-1999 in Patagonia.